Overhearing
the
Gospel

Also by Fred B. Craddock from Chalice Press:

As One Without Authority
(Fourth edition)

Craddock Stories
(edited by Mike Graves and Richard F. Ward)

REVISED AND EXPANDED

Overhearing
the
Gospel

FRED B. CRADDOCK

CHALICE™
PRESS
ST. LOUIS, MISSOURI

Cover art: © Artville, LLC
Cover and interior design: Elizabeth Wright
Art direction: Elizabeth Wright

This book is printed on acid-free, recycled paper.

Visit Chalice Press on the World Wide Web at
www.chalicepress.com

10 9 8 7 6 5 4 3 2 1   02 03 04 05 06 07

Library of Congress Cataloging–in–Publication Data

(Pending)

Printed in the United States of America

Contents

Preface to the First Edition

I feel I owe you a word about the context in which these reflections occurred. Perhaps this sense of obligation arises out of a reaction to some experience of a teacher or preacher who privately arrived at a conclusion that I was to accept immediately upon delivery, with no clue as to the whence, whither, or why of the speaker's journey. It may be that I have so often urged students to "build the nest before you lay the egg" that I dare not face them having bypassed my own counsel. Or maybe I know that the more perceptive readers will catch in mood and echo some very un-Oklahoma sights and sounds that subtly form the penumbra of these paragraphs (I thought and now write with surf pounding, sea gulls squawking, clam diggers bending over low tide, cottages nesting on islands in the sun, and crackling fire sending blue signals above the snow), and they will wonder whether I have been carried away, or should be.

Having been granted that change of pace and place that Phillips University called a research leave and that Yale University called a research fellowship, Nettie and I leased a cottage on Great Harbor off Old Sachem Head in Guilford, Connecticut. The cottage served for a time as a retreat because the work to which I was and am committed had, for a number of reasons, lost its edge, lying dull and heavy on my mind. There was nothing, thank goodness, of that terrible emptiness observed in some teachers and preachers who, while still carried along by the momentum of their profession, have lost appetite and replace it with cynicism. If anything, I am more and more moved and awed, even frightened, by the importance of teaching. But even so, it is possible to be immobilized now and then by the sense of how difficult it is and how small, at least apparently, are the gains we make. When this happens, it seems wise to back off in order to gather the advantages of distance. In other words, retreat.

But not for long. The time soon comes for inviting guests to the cottage to talk of teaching and preaching, of communicating the Christian message. It is important to have guests who have themselves faced the ponderous problem: How can we teach those who already know? How can we preach to those who have already heard? You who continue to read will observe in quotation and footnote the quality of those who shared with me in these conversations. But by far the most noticeable presence was Søren Kierkegaard. The text will reflect that of all the visitors, he came earliest and stayed latest. Never have I had a guest in my mind more delightful and stimulating. But he was not easy company. He was of such capacities of intellect and imagination that he often pushed the rest of us to the margins of the manuscript. More than once I had to remind myself that this was to be a book not about Kierkegaard but about a subject central to his life and to mine. In the pursuit of that subject, any person who can bring lively new ways of thinking and speaking to a church grown cynical about its own lectern and pulpit; any person who can move in on our vague and sterile concepts with a language of imaginative elasticity; any person who can offer an alternative to the predictably dull patterns of studying, speaking, and listening beyond which few of us have ventured; any person who has the grace to restrain the display of knowledge in order to evoke and increase my own; any person who, instead of simply adding increments to my knowledge, awakens in me the sense of having already known; any person who can bring to our heavy business the delights of wit and humor and the pathos of personal investment; that person is always welcome in my cottage, even if his presence is a judgment on my own dull efforts.

To Dean Joe R. Jones and the Graduate Seminary of Phillips University, I am grateful for this time of study and reflection. To Dean Colin Williams and Yale Divinity School, I am doubly grateful: for the invitation to spend a year enjoying that wealth of resources in library and faculty that is Yale and for the high honor of returning as Lyman Beecher Lecturer for 1978.

Fred B. Craddock
Enid, Oklahoma
February, 1978

Part I

The Illusion

1

Concerning Method

There is no lack of information in a Christian land;
something else is lacking, and this is a something which the
one cannot directly communicate to the other.

—SØREN KIERKEGAARD

I suppose you could say this statement from Kierkegaard is my text for the discussion that follows. As such, it is a radical departure from old custom and deep conviction, which have invariably dictated that if a text be used for a Christian discourse, it must be drawn from Holy Scripture. After all, what else is a sermon, or the whole of theology for that matter, but the continuation of the biblical discourse, engaging and being engaged by the ancient text? But I have granted myself an indulgence in this instance, because what follows is neither sermon nor theology.

Elevating a passage to the level of "text" does not mean passively accepting it as unqualified truth, to be served only by elaborations, applications, and exhortations. If with the sacred text one wrestles and grasps with the tenacity of Jacob—"I will not let

3

you go until you bless me"—one can be no less vigorous when engaging Kierkegaard. He delights in picking a fight with his reader, loading his sentences with exaggeration, humor, irony, sarcasm, and homely analogy, offering with one hand what he takes away with the other. So in the ways that a text properly functions—provoking thought and reassessment of old convictions, confirming prior wisdom while serving as governing consideration for new reflection and action—this statement is my text. Phrases within it will prompt our discussions to move in many directions, but its greatest single impact will come in its continually raising the question that refuses to leave the room all the time we are talking: How does one person communicate the Christian faith to another?

But that question itself already hinders us, arousing a widespread notion that threatens to abort fruitful discussion. The threat lurks in a general feeling about the word *how*. *How* is for many an ugly word, a cause of embarrassment. There is large opinion that *how* is to be found not among the prophets or the philosophers, but among mechanics and carpenters. After all, does not *how* introduce methods and skills more appropriate to a course in driver training than to probing into the mysteries of ultimate reality? What has skill to do with the kingdom of God? Kierkegaard sensed some of this condescension among the clergy and regarded it as a major cause for the decline in the quality of preaching. Perhaps no word among us has suffered more abuse than *how*, not the honorable abuse of attack, but the humiliating abuse of inattention, disregard, slight. *How* has been made to stand out in the hall while *what* was being entertained by the brightest minds among us. What is the issue? What is the truth? What do we believe? What is being taught? Those are the worthy questions, and who would suffer the embarrassment of interrupting the discussion with "But how can we...?" This arrogant dismissal of all considerations of method could properly draw the fire that Somerset Maugham intended for certain haughty devotees of culture among his acquaintances:

> Who has not seen the scholar's thin-lipped smile when he
> corrects a misquotation and the connoisseur's pained look
> when someone praises a picture he does not care for? There
> is no more merit in having read a thousand books than in
> having ploughed a thousand fields. There is no more merit

in being able to attach a correct description to a picture than in being able to find out what is wrong with a stalled motorcar. In each case it is special knowledge. The stockbroker has his knowledge too and so has the artisan. It is a silly prejudice of the intellectual that his is the only one that counts. The True, the Good, and the Beautiful are not perquisites of those who have been to expensive schools, burrowed in libraries and frequented museums. The artist has no excuse when he uses others with condescension. He is a fool if he thinks his knowledge is more important than theirs and an oaf if he cannot comfortably meet them on an equal footing.[1]

If this language is too strong for our present consideration, then at least it can register the intensity of my feelings when I survey the devastation wrought by an arrogant dismissal of method in our churches, colleges, and seminaries. Countless young men and women, graduates of excellent schools and of unquestioned intelligence and commitment, are paralyzed early in their ministries because in those tasks that are ministry, in the only sense that really matters, they do not know the how. Of course, there have always been those who insisted on preparation in the how of teaching, preaching, worship, and administration, but the long struggle upstream against the heavily theoretical curriculum tended to make some of them so reactionary and defensive that those of us who had been of a mind to champion their cause grew suspicious of what seemed to be anti-intellectual, nonsubstantive, shallow, and faddish. And these symptoms, in turn, reconfirmed and reinforced the original low opinion of programs centering on method. But the quarrel over the stature of the question *how?* and whether it deserved a place among the tall questions of our faith was radically shifted by my listening to Kierkegaard. He wrote thirty-five books, all of them in pursuit of a how: how to be a Christian, here in this place, now at this time. As the profundity and significance of those books testify, the pursuit of that question leads one not away from but deeper into the great issues of church history, theology, ethics, and scripture. I grow more and more convinced that the total curriculum of the church, from Sunday school to seminary, should wrestle with the Christian faith as *how*. Every *what* deserves consideration only as it serves the overarching question of how to be Christian.

Nevertheless, concern with how to be a Christian can sink into private rituals of self-probing, self-accusation, and self-approbation unless a prior question is faced and met with attempts at solution. That question has already been raised: How can one person communicate the Christian faith to another? As we reflect on the surpassing importance of this question, it is amazing that our condescension toward "how to do it" has not long since been overcome. I say "our" because I am by no means innocent. In graduate school, the program of study operated on the assumption that mastery of the subject matter of my field qualified me to teach in that field. Not only did I voice no complaint about this arrangement, I would have been incensed if my advisors had urged that, in view of my intention to teach, I learn something about teaching. How dare anyone dilute my *what* with a *how*!

I am speaking not simply as one who wishes to be a more effective communicator; I have another field of endeavor in which I work daily: listening. This is by far the more difficult, and I hope it is not pure unadulterated selfishness on my part to wish that those communicating to me would give more attention to how, to method, to style. Some listeners in churches have accepted boredom as one of the crosses that come with the commitment, but I cannot.

The issue is not one of simply being gracious in an unpleasant situation. Boredom is not just a condition that prompts humorous stories about this stale professor or that dull preacher. Boredom is a form of evil; perhaps one of Kierkegaard's characters was more correct when he said, "Boredom is the root of all evil."[2] Boredom is a preview of death, if not itself a form of death, and when trapped in prolonged boredom, even the most saintly of us will hope for, pray for, or even engineer relief, however demonic. Sincere Sunday worshipers will confess to welcoming in muffled celebration any interruption of the funereal droning. Be honest: Have you ever quietly cheered when a child fell off a pew or a bird flew in a window or the lights went out or the organ wheezed or the sound system picked up police calls or a dog came down the aisle and curled up to sleep below the pulpit? Passengers on cruise ships, after nine beautiful sunsets and eighty-six invigorating games of shuffleboard, begin to ask the crew hopefully, "Do you think we will have a storm?"

Recently I heard a quiet and passive clergyman tell of his attending the Indianapolis 500. He confessed that after two hours of watching the same cars speed by again and again, the boredom turned him into a degenerate sinner. At first, he said, he simply entertained thoughts of "What if...?" and his own imagination thrilled him. But soon his boredom demanded more. A car caught fire. Hoorah! Not until later did he remind himself that he, a Christian minister, had experienced no concern for the driver. But a burning car was not enough; something more dramatic was needed to effect a resurrection from the death of boredom. Voices within him, he admitted, began to call for a smashup. The demon of boredom had totally transformed him. Shift the scene to a classroom or sanctuary, subject him or you or me to repeated and prolonged boredom, and a similar process begins. For the communicating of the Christian faith, formally or informally, to be boring is not simply "too bad," to be glossed over with the usual "but he is really a genuine fellow" or "but she is very sincere." Boredom works against the faith by provoking contrary thoughts or lulling to sleep or draping the whole occasion with a pall of indifference and unimportance.

Now, I am as quick as you are to come up with reasons why the burden of boredom does not lie solely on the one speaking. The variables are many and certainly are factors in the case: room temperature, time of day or night, physical and mental state of the listeners, and so forth. But after we have completed our lists, scattered the blame lightly over three dozen possible causes, and assured one another that we will take them all into account, especially when holding postmortems over our own failures, should we not then accept a large share of responsibility for the condition and move on?

What is it that sustains the illusion that the Christian faith can proceed effectively without giving prime time or our best intelligence to such lesser considerations as method and style of communicating? The illusion seems to be fed by several fictions that have been naïvely embraced as the truth about how things are and are to remain. One such fiction is the formula widely accepted though seldom voiced that prescribes that attention to method, form, and style will be in inverse ratio to the importance of the subject matter. For example, if the subject is a new brand of barbecue sauce, not exactly a matter of transcendent importance, the speaker will not open his mouth until full and thrice-checked attention to details of method and style have been made. But suppose the subject is the Christian gospel; are we not to assume that the sheer weight of its significance is its own style, cutting a clear path straight to the hearer's mind and heart, and hence poorly served by any consideration that the speaker might give to appropriate form and method? As a matter of fact, many listeners entertain some suspicion of a speaker's sincerity if it is sensed that there has crept into the presentation a modicum of attention to the most effective method for communicating. Let the salesperson be lively and brilliant with a bar of soap, but let the person who speaks to and for the church be neither lively nor brilliant. There is no place for the charlatan in the kingdom!

In those academic circles where those who teach and preach receive their education, this same fiction about important matters needing no support from communicative arts is sustained in a way only slightly different from the above. In these circles, the preoccupation is with the truth. Of course, no one regards this as other than laudable, for where else is truth to be pursued with such objectivity, with such disregard for party interests or personal gain? Here the sober facts about life are handled with an imperturbability that could strike a casual observer as total indifference. It has to be; success in the educational endeavor demands adequate isolation from bombarding interests and distracting concerns about consequence and relevance. The basic assumption here is simply this: If the issue of all serious study is the truth, if we can find the truth, then no one need be further concerned with how to relate this truth to human life or human life to the truth. Once the truth is known, personal and communal appropriation of it will follow as naturally as night follows day.

That such is simply not the case is a realization painfully gained. The burden of it is expressed in the text from Kierkegaard: "There is no lack of information in a Christian land; something else is lacking." Kierkegaard's whole literary activity takes the measure of that immense gulf between concept and capacity. It is one thing to talk about a concept such as love, and quite another to have the capacity to love. And the one does not lead directly to the other. Knowledge about ethical concepts does not make one ethical. Burghardt DuBois, a great African American educator, sociologist, and historian, upon completion of studies at Fisk University, Harvard University, and the University of Berlin, was convinced that change in the condition of the African American could be effected by careful scientific investigations into the truth about the African American in America. So he proceeded. His research was flawless, and his graphs and charts impeccable. After waiting several years and hearing not the slightest stir of reform, DuBois had to accept the truth about the truth: Its being available does not mean it will be appropriated.

This does not mean that we should pause here and hurl charges against the general public for its blind indifference to higher values in its low pursuit of the thrills of pop culture. Maybe the theologians among us wish to speak here about original sin. Whatever the cause, the plain fact is, it is a tragic error to assume that the truth is its own evangelist. Whoever thinks that "telling them the truth" is all that is necessary to dispel human ills is going to spend a great deal of time shaking dust off the feet and traveling. You and I should face it: speeches on the transcendent values of ultimate reality can be awfully dull. As Kierkegaard put it, "Truth is not nimble on its feet"; it can be heavy-footed and pedestrian. And those of us concerned with communicating the Christian gospel, while confessing to the intrinsic adequacy of the message for salvation, must all the while follow the operational principle, if it has been heard. To effect that hearing is no small task.

The line of thinking productive of the errors discussed above presupposes an even more widespread fiction in our culture, that content and form of expression are separate considerations. Wherever this assumption exists, almost invariably content is on the inside and style on the outside; content is essential, and form is accessory, optional. It is supposed that matter and manner are separate entities, as though one has a message that, incidentally, is then expressed in a poem, or a historical event that just happens to then be cast into a story. Not so. How a speaker or singer or artist does is no subordinate dimension of what he or she does. How they do is what they do, and what they do is how they do it. A song is a song, a story is a story, a syllogism is a syllogism, and a parable is a parable.

For instance, analyze a parable to ascertain its meaning, dispense with the parabolic form, state its message as a proposition, and you have altered not just the how but also the what. Another case in point is the gospel. A gospel is a form as well as a message; it is a narrative conveying a sense of historical chronology and continuity, naming places and times and characters. That particular form of communicating is saying something important about the life of faith, and it is something quite different from a proverb or paradox or poem. Or permit a homely analogy. Have you ever noticed how much of what we experience is shaped by the anticipation of how we will share it with someone? You did not listen across the Austrian Alps for the fivefold echo of your own "hello," you did not coax your daughter into her very first step, you did not lean against the rail and stare into the fog for the first glimpse of the Statue of Liberty, and then sometime later think of communicating the experience. Were you not at the very time of the experiences already searching for words, phrases, analogies to go into the journal, the letter, the phone call? How experiences are communicated is a major factor in defining what those experiences are. There is no surgery—literary, logical, or experiential—by which what and how can be severed.

Even more regrettable, however, than the thought that style of expression would be regarded as separate from, subsequent and accessory to content, is that style would be viewed negatively, at best unnecessary embroidery on the truth and at worst subversion of it. You and I know that there is always style in communication. The bare and chaste description of a scientific undertaking is a style. But unfortunately, the word *style* enters our conversations only when there is a flourish, a flair, a noticeable artistry in the communication, and then sober brows denounce it as an intruder, a detractor. Of course, that can be and often is the case, and our highest and best thoughts suffer rather than profit from such glare and gloss. As Somerset Maugham said of certain writers,

> Their flashy effects distract the mind. They destroy their persuasiveness; you would not believe a man was very intent on ploughing a furrow if he carried a hoop with him and jumped through it at every other step.[3]

But all extremes and distortions aside, we still have a problem: "How is one to exorcise the feeling that 'style,' which functions like the notion of form, subverts content?"[4] We are still haunted by the ancient fear that style, especially attention to artistic form, compromises truth and morality. Ezekiel, prophet of the vivid image and metaphor, complained that the people took him lightly, as an interesting storyteller, a singer of beautiful songs (Ezek. 20:49; 33:32). In *Divine Hymns and Poems,* a volume for the church published in London in 1704, the editors devoted a lengthy preface warning all Christians of the dangers of poetry that, as is said of the siren's song, "While it charms it kills us." In a paragraph that could easily be enlarged to cover interest in form and style in all communication, the readers are sternly lectured:

> Vice is a deformed and odious thing, and if exposed naked would have but few admirers; it owes all its lustre to false colours, and these it chiefly borrows from the poets; 'tis they that smooth the monster's brow, and make her smile, that conceal her defects, and set her off to the greatest advantage. How many, who would have started at the open face of vice, have been enticed into its fatal embrace by means of those bewitching disguises that poetry has bestowed on it?[5]

It is because this warning contains some undisputed truth about the twisted uses of form and style to disguise and beguile that it has gained acceptance as a general truth about all effort after effective technique. Such acceptance erects a formidable barrier to progress in dealing seriously with the question, How can one person effectively communicate the Christian faith to another?

As an indication of how nervous most of us get when discussing method, here I am already feeling the need—and I hate that I do—to reassure the reader that none of these comments are to be construed as depreciation of content. Let us confirm one another at this point in the conviction that it does matter extremely what is said and what is heard. The question each generation has addressed to the desk, the pulpit, and the lectern of the church is, in William Temple's famous line, not "What will Jones swallow?" but "Is there anything to eat?" My own church tradition has often reminded its classrooms and sanctuaries that it is not in chewing but in chewing food that we are nourished.

But having paused to affirm the *what* of our communicating, I must return to our subject and repeat the insistence on effective form and style. Our task is not just to say the word and to tell the truth, but to get the truth heard, to effect a new hearing of the word among those who have been repeatedly exposed to it. Without that hearing, glorious claims for content and substance remain functionally theoretical, boasts of ore as yet unmined. Undoubtedly there are many powerful and life-changing ideas lying impotent in pale paragraphs and slipping unheard past bored ears, written and spoken by great thinkers who had no time or interest to give to such marginal matters as how one person communicates to another. On the other hand, who can deny that much of the lasting power of Nietzsche's philosophy is owed to his vivid and effective style? We tend to praise as "original" that thinking that comes to us in such a way as to get our attention.

Since we have paused to remind one another of misunderstandings that may arise when we heavily underscore or totally neglect style or method, we might as well be clear on another related matter. It is not to be assumed that the gospel provides religious and moral constraints on what we say but leaves how we say it to be governed solely by practical considerations of effectiveness. This simply is not true. I am sure all of us have had the experience of coming under the smiling attack of a sidewalk witness, overwhelming us with well-worn clichés and scripture fragments. Perhaps we were left speechless—sputtering sounds of anger, confusion—with a sense of having been violated. Very likely the primary cause of our being so disturbed was not the content of what was said, even if the biblical exegesis and theological perspective left much to be desired. Then why was the whole experience so blatantly and grossly unchristian, regardless of the amount of scripture quoted and the witness' assurance that we are loved? Because of the method by which the message came, because we know almost instinctively that if the province of the gospel does not include manner as well as matter, music as well as words, then we are not interested. Vague as it may seem at first, there is such a thing as appropriate style, a style that fits, a style that is a part of the very fabric of an occasion, of a relationship, of an event, of the truth. We recognize it when it is present, and we are so aware of its absence that we may have no choice but to stomp out of the room to escape the insult, even if that room be a sanctuary. There is such a thing as a Christian style, a method of communicating congenial to the nature of the Christian faith. As Brian Wicker has stated, "To say a story is a Christian story is to speak not just of its content but of its structure."[6]

I feel, then, the burden to work unceasingly at how to communicate. This burden is not laid on me simply by the practical concern to remain employed (a benefit not unwelcome) but by the nature of the gospel and of the call to effect a hearing of that gospel. All attempts to rid myself of this burden—I never had a way with words; a person should not be fancy with the truth; style is for novelists and poets, but I am a preacher; I just tell it like it is, and if they miss it, that is their problem—have been quite unsuccessful. *How* is a question that will not leave. If I toss it out the door with loud disclaimers that style is a matter of art and that I am without such gifts, it returns through the window, quietly but firmly reminding me that "art is not a gift which a few people are given, but rather it is a gift which most people throw away."

The way to begin, for all of us, is to recognize and to accept the complexity and the difficulty of communicating. We read a book by an author for whom it seems so effortless; we hear a lecturer or preacher who seems to float along on natural gifts. We ask "how?" and they all speak of work, work, work. Some flashes, to be sure, but usually working without ecstasy. The difficulties are there, whether preparing for formal presentations or simply negotiating the normal flow of human relations. All sensitive persons have more than once been reduced to quivering silence, mute before the unexpected gift, mute beside the bereaved friend, mute at the table with a hurt and alienated son. The difficulties of communicating were there long before we began wrestling with law and gospel, judgment and grace, time and eternity, bondage and freedom, myth and history, exegesis and hermeneutics. It is one of the painful discoveries of childhood that there are powerful forces that isolate us one from the other, forces that persuade us to be safely silent rather than hurling a word against the enclosing glass that ensures our privacy.

> As a boy, I spent pleasant summer evenings gathering fallen stars. As I think back on it, the spent stars were worthless, but it was something to do. My brothers and I would go into a field near the house, climb up on tree stumps (all that remained after the blight of a once beautiful chestnut grove), and wait for stars to fall. From these perches we could see exactly where they fell, and it was not uncommon to have our pockets filled within an hour. Sometimes, whether in greed or out of compassion for fallen stars that might otherwise go unnoticed, I do not know, we would sneak from the back porch with Grandma's clothes basket and harvest the remaining stars still flickering on the ground. And sometimes, dragging the heavy basket home left us too tired to empty it. "We will do it in the morning," but in the morning Grandma was already fussing about a residue of gray ashes in her

clothes basket. (Everyone knows you cannot save stars over until the next night.) We denied charges of having kindled a fire in her basket and snickered off to play, protected from punishment by the mystery. But during her last illness, Grandma called me to her bed and told me, almost secretively, that she knew what we had been doing with her basket. My guilty silence was broken by her instruction for me to bring to her from the bottom of an old chest a package wrapped in newspaper. I obeyed and then waited the eternity it took for her arthritic fingers to open the bundle. "Oh, it's gone," she said, showing me where it had been. In the bottom of the package was a little residue of gray ashes. We stared at each other.

"You too, Grandma? Why didn't you tell me?"

"I was afraid you would laugh at me. And why didn't you tell me?"

"I was afraid you would scold me."

Multiply sevenfold the awkwardness, the pain, the obstacles in that simple scene, and we are in the frame of mind to entertain our central question: How? How can one person communicate the gospel to another? When Kierkegaard began seriously to wrestle with that question, he saw immediately that his efforts would be futile unless he faced squarely the condition before him. That condition he came to describe most frequently as "a monstrous illusion." According to his diagnosis of the spiritual state of Denmark, "There is no lack of information in a Christian land; something else is lacking." On the basis of that assessment, Kierkegaard developed his method of communication. Any appropriateness of his method for us depends to a large extent on the correspondence between his situation and our own.

We have explored something of the shape and nature of the illusion surrounding considerations of style. According to Kierkegaard, an even more forbidding illusion surrounds the listener "in a Christian land." To this subject we now turn.

2

Concerning the Listener

*There is no lack of information in a Christian land;
something else is lacking.*

Discussing teaching and preaching with Kierkegaard has made
me wonder if perhaps I have tended to idealize my listeners in
both classroom and sanctuary. I think I have, and on reflection, it
may not have been such a bad thing; it may have saved me from
the deadly cynicism that has dragged down good friends of proven
ability in lecture and sermon. By idealizing I mean simply that I
have stood in pulpits with the image of listeners as hungry and
thirsty, one question pushing aside all others: How can I be a
Christian? I have entered seminary classrooms challenged and
yet comforted by what seemed a proper assumption: These young
men and women are impelled by one governing consideration,
thorough preparation for Christian ministry. If I exaggerate, it is
only slightly, and frankly, it is my hope that repeated exposures
to the "grim realities" will not alter measurably this approach to
any group of listeners or learners. To be sure, there are listeners to
sermons whose minds are off and running after questions other

than the morning topic, questions such as: What shall we eat? What shall we drink? With what shall we be clothed? and When does this service end? Of course, there are students who are motivated by likes and dislikes, who comb through bibliographies seeking not the best books but those with fewest pages and largest print, who live by the eleventh commandment, Thou shalt barely get by. But is it not the wiser policy to address the best and highest in listeners and hope for what can be? No acceptable alternative comes to mind.

Nevertheless, neither idealism on one hand nor cynicism on the other may actually contribute anything specifically to the task of communicating. In fact, either attitude may serve as excuse for not working diligently at the *how* of teaching and preaching. The idealist may say, "Regardless of my method in sharing this matter, they are hungry and will consume it immediately." The cynic may say, "It does not matter how much I prepare, they are not interested." Needless to say, whether smiling or frowning, excuses are excuses and always carry within them the seeds of death to the whole enterprise.

But let us move in more closely. Forget the cynic; nothing is more fruitless and futile and foreign to the gospel than cynicism. Assume we approach our listeners with a strong and positive will to communicate. Now let us ask one question about the hearer. What factor in the listener's condition erects the greatest obstacle to the hearing of the message? Perhaps an answer lies immediately before us.

"In a Christian land." In that apparently positive and welcome phrase lurks the problem. Insofar as the hindrance to communication can be located in the condition of the hearer, here it is. In circumstances so obviously favorable to the gospel that one can use an expression such as "Christian land," there can flourish the illusion of participation where little or none actually exists.

"In a Christian land." You and I are not sharing the gospel as pioneer missionaries chopping our way through the jungle to bring the fresh, new, first-time word to startled villagers. Perhaps most of us have in times of disappointment wished it were so, idealizing such occasions as opportunities to write the message on new tablets. Of course, there are no new targets; those that appear to be are really palimpsests, already covered with earlier scribblings.

This is what Paul, who made it his aim to preach where the gospel had never been heard, discovered to his constant exasperation.

But what Paul's listeners brought to a first Christian worship service is only slightly similar to the burden of my hearers. Those who hear me have been sitting before the pulpit for two thousand years. Even for the casual listeners there is a fairly high degree of predictability in the sermon, and surrounding the whole occasion is the dead air of familiarity, "We have been here before, and here we go again." I do not wish to argue here that Christendom still prevails in this country as a whole. Nevertheless, the basic presuppositions and values of that portion of society to which I expose the gospel are traditionally Christian. Those to whom I speak are, as a rule, persons who often hear sermons, attend worship, and generally find themselves at home in the language, rituals, and teachings of the Christian faith. Not only are chances very good that they will say even of good sermons that they have heard it all before, but if what they hear is different from what they have been accustomed to hearing, in manner or in matter, they will suspect that it was not a sermon or not Christian.

Even more strikingly similar to Christendom is the other context in which I attempt to communicate the Word and its implication—the theological seminary. Students in a seminary have a steady diet, together and separately, formally and informally, of Bible, theology, church history, ethics, and ministerial practice. It is assumed by administration, faculty, and students that all are Christian, having embraced the subject matter in that personal appropriation we call faith. So here they are before me, having already studied in the area of my discipline, having just come from a course in theology and soon to be on their way to a class in Old Testament or church history. What is my task? More increments of information? No doubt, this is one proper expectation. But how much more pressing, albeit much more difficult, is the challenge to help them to hear what they hear every day, to learn what they already know, to be apprehended by that material with which exams are passed.

If the New Testament provides us a model, it is not Paul, who spoke primarily to those for whom the gospel was a first-time experience, but Jesus, whose listeners were up to their ears in scripture—rabbis, scribes, and priests—and who had also been sitting before pulpits for a thousand years. It is with his burden I identify: to enable a new hearing and, quite possibly, a hearing for the very first time. It is abundantly clear in the gospels that Jesus as a communicator employed methods to overcome the major obstacle to hearing in his audience: in a context of long tradition, common assumptions, and high predictability in messages, there is much room for the illusion of participation where little or none exists. Many who say "Here we go again" have not in fact ever gone before. I do not say this to be critical or to cast doubt on anyone's sincerity. We are up against an illusion that breeds in the dark, unswept corners of institutions well furnished by custom, repetition, and assumption. And the task of any communicator who would seek to shatter this illusion is made doubly difficult by the fact that victims of an illusion do not realize they are victims. On the contrary, such a charge by a speaker would likely meet strong protest and angry denial. Such is the nature of an illusion: it caresses; there is no pain. It is the communicator who succeeds in breaking the illusion who brings pain, who is the troubler in Israel. I realize that I speak here of degrees, for all of us have learned to survive by having a partial deafness and blindness to the real condition of ourselves and of our world. "If we had a keen vision and feeling of all ordinary human life, it would be like hearing the grass grow and the squirrel's heart beat, and we should die of that roar which lies on the other side of silence. As it is, the quickest of us walk about well wadded with stupidity."[1] But the truth in this observation about "the quickest of us" must not be taken as relief from the assignment to try to reach those so "well wadded" by a kind of Christendom that their real spiritual state is obscured by the indolence of habit.

Kierkegaard should be able to help us. He really did live in Christendom, in a Christian land, and in that context he sensed as keenly as anyone that "something else is lacking." Church and state in Denmark were joined in the concord that provided tax support for the church, government salaries for ministers, and that broad practice of baptism that made citizenship in the country and membership in the church one covenant. Even after we have discounted the differences between the Danish church in the nineteenth century and that circle of listeners who attend to our efforts, hearing him describe his situation brings uncomfortably to mind not differences but similarities. Listen to him in a selection of comments that I hope have not been distorted by removing them from various writings:

Everyone with some capacity for observation, who seriously considers what is called Christendom, or the conditions in a so-called Christian country, must surely be assailed by profound misgivings. What does it mean that all these thousands and thousands call themselves Christians as a matter of course?[2]

We all of us indeed are Christians. But with this what have we all become, I wonder; and what has Christianity become by the fact that we all of us as a matter of course are Christians of a sort?[3]

When I am not a Christian and confront the decision of becoming one, Christianity helps me to an acute aware-ness of the decision...But when it is as if the matter were already decided...there is nothing in the external situation to arouse in me an awareness of the decision. On the contrary, there is something that tends to prevent me from having my attention called to it (and this is the factor that increases the difficulty), namely, that the decision has apparently already been made. In brief, it is easier to become a Christian when I am not a Christian than to become a Christian when I am one.[4]

One has only to let the mind remain poised over this condition for a few moments of reflection to grasp some of the monstrous proportions and demonic results of this prodigious illusion. The church, coextensive with the state, found herself both villain and victim. Lulled into fat slumber by the size of her membership and purse, her message suffered from the acoustical illusion that the voice of the people was the voice of God. Mesmerized by the optical illusion of her splendor mirrored in grand buildings, her prophetic discernment gave way to concern for the apparent. To characterize this concern for appearances, Kierkegaard often used the analogy of wearing a wig. Our age, he said, has sold its trousers to buy a wig.[5]

The church did, of course, continue to speak and to write under these conditions, but the gospel had become, Kierkegaard lamented, a "piece of information." Passion was replaced by descriptions of passion. The net effect for the church, said Kierkegaard, could be compared with reading from a cookbook to a man who is hungry. Theological discussions became intramural games played within conceptual systems closed in their own logic and consistency unresponsive to new experience, personal and social. It was an age of deliberation and reflection, caught up in the seductive sophistication of entertaining the theoretical, wrote Kierkegaard. He played with the idea of preparing a statistical table displaying the annual consumption of intelligence in Denmark, just as others had prepared on the annual consumption of liquor. But there was no action. An assembly might be called for purposes of entertaining the idea of academic or religious or political revolt, and after lively discussion, all could go home satisfied with the evening. And as assurance that the high quality of these gatherings would continue, all competitively shared little stories of early evidence of the precocity of their children.[6]

All this took place under the illusion that if the discussion is religious or theological in content, the occasion is Christian. But this is far from the truth. The apostle Paul can be the topic of conversation, but that alone does not merit calling the discussion either biblical or Christian. It was, and in some circles remains, fashionable to speak of Paul as brilliant and a genius, but to entertain Paul as a profound thinker is far different from listening to him as an apostle. In fact, there can be in such occasions ostensibly theological and Christian in substance, the very contradiction of the gospel. Kierkegaard understood quite well that there can be at work in these exercises a kind of imperialism of the mind in which the thinkers are in control of the subject matter, at times contracting it into syllogisms and at others expanding it into philosophical worldviews. The bright young minds attracted to this probing love the mastery of ideas that excite the intellect. In the process, however, it is forgotten that "the point of religious language is...to stimulate the process of experience and thought which will re-constitute human personality."[7]

It is the respect and high esteem in which the church holds ideas and intellectual activity that often blind her to the hazards of allowing reflection and discussion to be her central business. Those of us who celebrate thinking can easily forget that it can be yet another way of avoiding life. As long as life can be kept at a distance by sticking to ideas and concepts, a clever head can clear the way to operate a brothel and publish a new hymnbook at the same time. It is when she is out of touch with the concrete particulars of any one person's experiences that the church concentrates her attention on truth in general, life in general, death in general. Attracted, and quite reasonably so, to the virtues and benefits of broad vision and healthy abstraction, the church can develop a pattern of teaching and preaching that assumes the listeners live in general and die in general. "Alas, while the speculative and worshipful Herr Professor is engaged in explaining the whole of existence, he has in distraction forgotten his own name: namely, that he is a human being, not a fantastic three-eighths of a paragraph."[8]

> It came to pass that there was a certain minister who preached to his little flock of "the world today," "modern man," and "the history of the race." A layman complained of not being addressed by the sermons, but his complaints were turned aside with admonitions against small-mindedness and provincialism. In the course of time, the minister and the layman attended together a church convention in a distant city. When the minister showed some anxiety about their losing their way in the large and busy metropolis, the layman assured him there was no reason to fear. With that word, he produced from the rear seat of the car a globe of the world.

One does not have to read about the church in Kierkegaard's Denmark to know what happens to preaching and teaching when the broad assumption is that all are Christian and need only to be confirmed in what they have already accepted in advance. The clergy predigests every morsel offered through lesson and sermon. The path of discipleship, lest it prove too difficult, is made monotonously smooth. The offense of the gospel, once faced by all those first hearers of the Nazarene, is now removed. The message no longer carries the paradox of God in flesh, placing the hearer in a position of risk and decision. On the contrary, the certainty of the faith is guaranteed by reminders of inspiration of scripture, infallibility of dogma, apostolic authority, and indisputable miracles. Christians need not bother themselves further about the hiddenness of God in nature or in history or in a crucifixion. Thanks to centuries of unbroken Christian tradition, ministers can now deliver sermons in which, even to indifferent listeners, God is as obvious as a very rare and tremendously large green bird with a red beak sitting in a tree on a mound, and perhaps even whistling in an unheard of manner, or maybe as compellingly apparent as the figure of a man eighteen feet tall.[9]

Thus, in the world of Kierkegaard, the Christian faith reposed in the indolence of habit. The risk of faith was gone. "To whom shall we go?" and "Are you he, or shall we look for another?" were now stupid questions. The struggle of faith was gone. Jacob no longer limped, and Gethsemane was bathed in light. The truth of faith was gone. It seems never to have occurred to the church leaders that "an idea becomes false and impotent when it seeks reconciliation, at cut-rate prices, with other ideas."[10] But there was "no lack of information," and the church copied it off and recited it by rote. There was success—were not all the people members?—and yet there was abysmal failure, as there always is where assumptions operate in the place of decision and personal investment. The listener in classroom and pew becomes the tragic victim of that illusion of participation where actually none exists, an illusion created by the power of sheer numbers to overwhelm private judgment and personal decision.

> I have not the least doubt that every single individual in the nation will be honest enough with God and with himself to say in solitary conversation, "If I must be candid, I do not deny that I am not a Christian in the New Testament sense"...I have not the least doubt that everyone will with respect to ten of his acquaintances, let us say, be able to hold fast to the view that they are not Christians in the New Testament sense...But when there are one hundred thousand, one becomes confused.[11]

In isolated cases of individuals taking time and occasion to reflect on their spiritual state, two forms of dissatisfaction appeared. Kierkegaard goes so directly to the heart of the matter that one almost forgets then and there and thinks here and now. On the one hand, he says, was the person plagued by a sense of uncertainty about his condition before God. Were he to express his anxiety openly, he would be smothered in angry glances and people would say, "How tiresome to make such a fuss about nothing at all; why can't he behave like the rest of us, who are all Christians? It is just as it is with F. F., who refuses to wear a hat on his head like others, but insists on dressing differently." And if he raised the question in private to his wife, no doubt she would respond with some exasperation, "How can you get such notions into your head? How can you doubt that you are a Christian? Are you not a Dane, and does not the geography say that the Lutheran form of the Christian religion is the ruling religion in Denmark? For you are surely not a Jew, nor are you a Mohammedan; what then can you be if not a Christian?"[12]

On the other hand was the person who plagued others with his sense of certainty about his own secure favor with God, a position from which he could easily observe the contrasting lack in others. The little huddle of believers about such a person nodded agreement with his scoldings, but those at whom they were aimed were not present and were not likely ever to be. Hence, his message was hardly more than gossip to one group about another. But this certain one might appear suddenly as a religious enthusiast, hurling voice and pen against the whole church, noisily denouncing in indiscriminate broadsides the institution, its leaders, and its members. Even if the truth were on his side, his extremity was his undoing. Watching the immobile mass of the middle of the church render him harmless was a comic tragedy. With little effort, even less imagination, and absolutely no penitence or soul-searching, such a fellow can be avoided, his mouthings ridiculed as uncouth, and his message denounced as heretic. Obviously this man, says the church, is one of those fanatics who does not appreciate all that the church has done to upgrade our culture and bring refinement to persons of taste. More frequently, however, as is still the case, these absolutely certain ones formed cells within the church, meeting often to remind themselves that they were not as other men and women. These people preserved their own pious place by shutting themselves up in small groups for mutual confirmation in the belief, perfectly obvious to themselves, that they were the only true Christians to be found in the country.[13]

But the mass of those who kept some contact with the church, neither from a sense of certainty nor uncertainty, but from habit or social pressure, what was their condition as listeners? From Kierkegaard's wealth of analogies and images, two come immediately to mind. He compares them to children of well-to-do parents who have never stopped to realize that their daily food is a gift. In fact, they refuse wholesome food because they have never been hungry, preferring sweets instead.[14] In another place, Kierkegaard compares this "Christian" to a man growing thinner day by day. The physician looks at his wasted frame and explains to the family that it is not a result of want. On the contrary, his sad condition has come from eating all the time, out of season, when not hungry, and thereby ruining his digestion to the point that he resembles a starving man.[15] So it is with the spiritual state of those who are always being fed but who have never had that prerequisite to good health—appetite. Those who hunger and thirst shall be filled. If it is the nature of grace that it can enter only empty space, those who are never empty must in the most tragic sense always be empty. "There is no lack of information...something else is lacking."

> In a certain village the school bell rang at 8:30 a.m. to call the children to class. The boys and girls left their homes and toys reluctantly, creeping like snails into the school, not late but not a second early. The bell rang again at 3:30 p.m., releasing the children to homes and toys, to which they rushed at the very moment of the tolling of the bell. This is how it was every day, with every child. Except one. She came early to help the teacher prepare room and materials for the day. She stayed late to help the teacher clean the board, dust erasers, and put away materials. And during the day she sat close to the teacher, all eyes and ears, for the lessons being taught. One day when noise and inattention were worse than usual, the teacher called the class to order. Pointing to the little girl in the front row, the teacher said, "Why can you not be as she is? She comes early to help, she stays late to help, and all day long she is attentive and courteous." "It isn't fair to ask us to be as she is," said one boy from the rear of the room. "Why?" "Because she has an advantage," he replied. "I don't understand. What is her advantage?" asked the puzzled teacher. "She is an orphan," he almost whispered as he sat down.

Am I to believe, as Kierkegaard did, that this lack of appetite, this starvation amid plenty, prevails before my pulpit and lectern, that over the years the illusion of participation has created the deadly atmosphere of high predictability and low expectation, so much so that communication is extremely difficult? Must I more realistically approach my work with the assumption that most are present by reason of habit, because of social pressure, or from some now-forgotten acquiescence, and that they have gathered expecting no more than repeated bits of information and a few familiar moral orders? That is a most frightening prospect, especially if one is neither of a mind to give up on anyone nor of a desire to take over the lives of those who have relinquished the right to do their own expecting, asking, searching, and risking.

That some such persons are in classrooms and sanctuary is clearly evident. Some church people seem simply and passively to want to be told what to think, what to believe, and what to do. Remember Franz Kafka's little parable "The Watchman"?

> I ran past the first watchman. Then I was horrified, ran back again and said to the watchman: "I ran through here while you were looking the other way." The watchman gazed ahead of him and said nothing. "I suppose I really oughtn't to have done it," I said. The watchman still said nothing. "Does your silence indicate permission to pass?"[16]

Have the preaching and teaching of the church helped shape such a person, who cowers at every intersection waiting for someone to say yes or no, or does the church speak so as to appeal primarily to persons already this way? Some are most certainly inquiring, struggling seekers after God, hoping for genuine appropriation of the word that will overcome the distance they feel between themselves and God. But so often the church has had little room for inquiring and struggling, making those so engaged feel guilty for so little faith. And in many places the church has given the impression that the distance from God can be negotiated, not by faith's wrestling, but by increments of information that the church can supply. Having gotten this impression, of course some listeners eagerly heap up texts, arrange biblical evidences, and sit before those teachers and preachers who answer such questions as, Where was Eden? Who wrote Genesis? What finally will happen to the Jews? Are spaceships mentioned in the Bible? and, Is Mount Ararat in Russia? Whatever claim these and similar questions have on our minds, you and I know that the conversion of the Christian faith into this game of questions and answers is a glib and shallow business. But many of our listeners engage in it with a flourish, and to refuse to play is to be charged with not knowing the Bible, not knowing Jesus Christ, and to be told softly and tenderly by some saccharine voice, "But we'll pray for you." I hate profanity, but I think I prefer the street variety to that veiled form that introduces the name of God so carelessly into ordinary prattle.

If this is a prevalent type of listener to us, the task of communication is indeed difficult. This listener is not ignorant in search of understanding, not hungry and thirsty, not groping in the darkness for the relief of a beam of light. No, he is familiar with churches, worship services, the Bible, study groups, and some religious literature; he can name his favorite preachers and teachers. And after years of those exposures, he has some questions: Where did Cain get his wife? Exactly where will we be five minutes after death? Does the Bible say the antichrist will be a leader of the United Nations?

And there is a good chance you will be asked one of these questions in a hallway, in a restaurant, on your way to the restroom, or at the cashier's counter in the supermarket. "Could you not inform me what an eternal happiness is, briefly, clearly, definitely? Could you describe it while I shave?"[17] This glib haste signals a distance between the inquirer and the message, but a distance hidden in the illusion of enthusiastic participation and "really knowing the Bible."

How shall we communicate in an atmosphere where it is assumed the gospel has been heard and that now all that remains is supplying more units of information? A husband and wife take hours and days and years to know each other, and yet some would know God before the parking meter expires. Lifetime questions take a lifetime; questions of conscience require conscience; issues of morals and religion can be handled only after one has achieved some size, some dimensions of pathos, sympathy, concern, and sensitivity. The wisdom tradition of the Old Testament and intertestamental period repeatedly insists that some things are not understood simply by the learned. There is an understanding peculiar to the righteous man, to the person who lives within an understanding distance of God. Ludwig Wittgenstein spoke of language being understood only within a certain form of life. C. S. Lewis in all his writings insisted on the relation of right thinking to right living.[18] In other words, in the final analysis listening is a quality of character. It is no wonder that those like Kierkegaard, who understand this, are rather reluctant to share the fruits of a lifetime of prayer and study and discipline with someone who wants to talk religion while waiting for the light to change. Kierkegaard once told of a man who was given the assignment of entertaining himself for an entire day; however, the man was such a clever fellow that he was finished by noon.[19] "There is no lack of information in Christian land; something else is lacking."

> There was once an old man whose only close friend was his dog. The love between them had deepened through the years. Now both had begun to feel the pain and burden of age. The dog, twelve years old, could hardly walk and was covered with an irritating rash. The old man lifted the dog in his arms and carried it to the car, where it lay on the seat beside him on the way to a veterinarian. From the parking lot the old man carried the dog gently inside. "Can I help you?" asked the veterinarian. The old man, still holding his dog, said, "First I must ask you a question. Do you love animals above everything else?" "Well, I love God first. Jesus says in Mark 12:30, 'You shall love the Lord your God with all your heart, and with all your soul, and with all your mind, and with all your strength.' And, of course a second command is to love the neighbor as oneself. We must put these things first, and then we can think about the animals." "Then I must go elsewhere," said the old man as he moved toward the door. "Why? What is wrong?" "This dog is my friend," explained the old man, "and I feel I can trust him only to the care of a veterinarian who is a Christian."

Perhaps by this time you are wondering if I have forgotten those listeners who are the good soil on whom the seed produces a harvest thirty-, sixty-, and one hundredfold. Certainly not. There are such participating listeners in classroom and sanctuary, and they are for all of us inspiration and challenge. It is not to be negative or critical that I give attention to the soil like the path, so often traveled and so hardened by repetition that it seems no longer receptive to the seed. It is rather to accept the challenge of communicating with these minds and hearts dulled by long and repeated exposure to the words and forms of the Christian faith. I am convinced that the listener we address is quite often living in the illusion of Christendom not too different from Kierkegaard's listener and reader. And this illusion is so believable: gatherings of people using traditionally Christian vocabulary, engaging in some traffic in biblical and theological information, meeting in sanctuaries and classrooms set aside for religious instruction, and led by those learned in the subject matter of the faith are therefore hearing and speaking the gospel. Please understand: Not for a moment would I eliminate such gatherings or change the subject matter. Such reactions against institutions and academic disciplines are nonsense. The point is, some who engage daily or weekly in Christian programs or discussions are not aware that no one is really engaged; something else is lacking. And others who are aware that something is lacking are often easy prey to those enthusiasts who make messianic claims for no structure, no agenda, no content, no tradition, no discipline.

These listeners are my present concern, these who through old habit have already agreed in advance of hearing and therefore do not hear. Then why not leave them alone? Because they too are victims, not of darkness, but of constant exposure to the same kind of light. They too have a right to hear what they have heard, see what they have seen, and understand what they have known.

But how can this be achieved? How can we speak or write for those of whom Kierkegaard said they already know too much? To enable hearers to walk down the corridors of their own minds, seeing anew old images hanging there, images that have served more powerfully than all concepts and generalizations in shaping them into the feeling, thinking, acting beings they are; to pronounce the old vocabulary so that someone hears a new cadence in it—that is the task here. But the teacher and preacher should not easily assume that the problem lies primarily with the listener. The listener's condition may be due in part to the fact that many of us who communicate the faith regularly find it more comfortable to stay in the warm circle of the familiar terms and phrases of our tradition, choosing not to push ourselves or our listeners out to what Paul van Buren calls "the edge of language." Sure, we want to communicate, but disturbances of the usual and predictable can be painful and costly. At the other extreme, we certainly resist the idea of being peddlers, willing to brighten the drab occasion and chase away monotony with sideshows and bargains. We are forewarned by Kierkegaard's innkeeper who, in reduced circumstances, did anything to attract customers, or by his portrait of the elderly man who sought to shake off the burden of age by decking himself out in the latest fashions of youth, only to feel embarrassed and out of place.[20] Then how?

Whatever the style or styles we develop in struggling with the *how* of our teaching and preaching, in no way can we permit our method to become elitist. It is an act of prejudgment—a denial of the efficacy of God's grace—and a contradiction of our mission to decide in advance who is the good soil and to withhold the seed from all others. Painful as it often is to share publicly and unreservedly that which through long incubation and nurture has come to be so personally our own, a lofty refusal to "waste my sweetness on the desert air" can never be an alternative. The gospel, not you or I, will create and determine its own listeners. Some decisions are not ours to make. I am continually learning this lesson from an experience remembered from shy and fearful adolescence. A pretty girl had moved into our town and into our school. She was immediately popular. Admiring her from a distance, I asked her, in the privacy of my mind, to go with me to the movies. I looked at her, then looked at myself, and in the privacy of my mind, she said no. For days afterward I was both hurt and angry at her rejection of me, a decision she was never allowed to make. It may be that when we speak to many, only a few will hear, but we have not been called to speak to a few and then complain that there are not many. Thoreau quietly resolved this issue in his now familiar pastoral reflection:

> I long ago lost a hound, a bay horse, and a turtle-dove, and am still on their trail. Many are the travelers I have spoken to concerning them, describing their tracks and what calls they answer to. I have met one or two who have heard the hound, and the tramp of the horse, and even seen the dove disappear behind a cloud, and they seemed as anxious to recover them as if they had lost them themselves.[21]

Perhaps among the listeners to lectures and sermons are those on whom the forces of negative adaptation have wrought the final tragedy: They have heard and heard and heard until now they cannot hear. Perhaps someone sits regularly before me who fits George Steiner's description: "He who has read Kafka's *Metamorphosis* and can look into his mirror unflinching may technically be able to read print, but is illiterate in the only sense that matters."[22] All this may be true, but we will proceed as though it were not. To slip into methods that assume such a condition would be to trap them and me in a self-fulfilling prophecy. To work at a way of communicating that assumes it is not true would be to—well, who knows?

But we are not yet ready to move to that consideration of method. We are in the process of seeking to understand the illusion that shrouds a traditionally Christian context and hinders communication. We are doing so by attempting to locate the "cannot" in Kierkegaard's statement: "There is no lack of information in a Christian land; something else is lacking and this is a something which the one cannot directly communicate to the other." We have found one fragment of this "cannot" in the low opinion of style among Christian communicators and another in the condition of the hearer who has been long and repeatedly exposed to the words and rites of the gospel. As has already been intimated, an exploration of the condition of the speaker should be equally fruitful. We now turn the investigation back on ourselves.

3

Concerning the Teller

*Something else is lacking, and this is a something which
the one cannot directly communicate to the other.*

We have been examining this statement from Kierkegaard,
trying to define the "lack" and locate the "cannot," all on the
assumption that the condition he faced as a communicator is
sufficiently like our own to make the investigation practical and
fruitful. Kierkegaard's summary term for describing that condition
was *illusion,* and he understood as well as anyone the difficulty of
breaking an illusion in order to communicate the Christian faith.
As we have seen, the illusion may surround the task of
communicating itself, creating the impression that form and
method are totally subordinate and extrinsic to the subject matter
of the Christian religion, the substance of which is of such weight
as to be poorly served by the embroidery of style. Or the illusion
may engulf the listener, giving the impression that there is
participation in the message when in fact there is only distance.
We come now to ask if the "something else lacking" is in any way

to be found in the speaker, if Kierkegaard's "cannot" is to some degree located in the mouth of the communicator and not just in the ear of the hearer. In other words, are those who teach and preach also caught in illusions, illusions about their own participation in what they say and in their relationship to those to whom they say it? For instance, some insist that distance both from the message shared and from the listeners is essential to professional competence; to participate personally in the subject matter and in the lives of those who hear tends to reduce the quality of one's work as a communicator. Is this true? We need to give our attention to this, not just now, but regularly in order to know who we are and what we are doing.

If Christianity may be called a story, what is the relationship of the teller to the story? The church has thought hard and long about this matter, and the discussion still goes on. It has insisted that some distance between message and messenger be not only permitted but urged for the sake of clear research and honest scholarship. The church has also insisted, in the face of constant misunderstanding, that the message should not be so closely tied to the life of the messenger that it appear that the efficacy of God's Word is contingent on the quality of character and faith in the messenger. God's power can be perfected even in weakness. In spite of all the frightening implications some might find in such a doctrine, we embrace it as true and Christian. But Kierkegaard has taught us anew that from the standpoint of effective communication of the Christian faith, distance between teller and story can be, finally, fatal. He listened every week to someone lecturing or preaching and witnessed all the evidences of the takeover of habit, custom, and familiarity. The relationship of the speaker to what he was saying was obviously quite casual. I have been confirmed by Kierkegaard in my own strong conviction that, whatever may be the talents displayed, the gospel is not communicated by sharing clippings and quotations. This is the work of hirelings, those who scour newspapers, magazines, and books for what can be used. Such is the sorry business of those who accept the role of consumer, quite happy to let scholars, poets, novelists, and even cartoonists be the producers. To this end come those who have lost the passion for their task and who now no longer preach or teach the gospel, but who drop the names of famous persons endorsing the product, extol the contributions of

Christianity to our civilization, urge attendance to ecclesiastical duties, and occasionally scold the absentees.

In contrast, Kierkegaard punctuated his descriptions of those who would be communicators of the Christian faith with such words as intensity, discipline, passion, pathos. It was in his day a commonly held notion that by means of the press Christian truth could quickly and easily be packaged and dispensed to the general public. In response to such a proposal, Kierkegaard put his central question:

> Dost thou venture even to maintain that "truth" can just as quickly be understood as falsehood, which requires no preliminary knowledge, no schooling, no discipline, no abstinence, no self-denial, no honest concern about oneself, no patient labour?[1]

It is important to understand what he is saying. He is not calling for something to replace careful study. Never. He knew as well as anyone that the speaker who capitulates to the notion that "analyzing it ruins it" has rendered to the listener a great disservice. Nor is Kierkegaard simply calling on teachers and preachers to be good examples in the exercise of religion. Rather, he is saying that the way to understand and to communicate the Christian faith is through disciplined participation in that faith. This is not an option for the communicator. How does one become qualified to talk of forgiveness, of penitence, of the death of Christ—read a good book on the subject? It is by obedience and sacrifice. Appropriation of the gospel is the minimum condition for approaching pulpit or podium. From the standpoint of the hearers, the qualities of the teller affect the response to the story. The decision that a message is worth listening to is a decision that the teller is worth listening to. If the speaker is not in his speaking, if his absence is evidenced by an overage of clichés, quotations, and secondary sources, the hearers feel deceived and deprived. Anyone could have said it. When we respond,we respond to someone.[2] Regardless of how strenuously one may argue the autonomy of a piece of literature, that a poem is a poem, a lecture is a lecture, and a sermon is a sermon, readers and hearers are unconvinced.

Again, let us be sure we understand the issue here. I am not using Kierkegaard to throw weight behind old advice about practicing what you preach. Rather, the point is that this discipline and patient submission to the Word are the way to gain access to the Word to be shared. Is it hard study? Yes. Is it prayer? Yes. Is it worship? Yes. Here Kierkegaard is not pointing the rest of us to the tortuous climb up Golgotha while he himself took the primrose path. Every morning he reconvinced himself of the reality of God. He brought his life under the authority of the scriptures, not just to use the sacred texts but in order that they make a difference in the way he thought on every subject. There may be isolated cases in which one could claim that attention or inattention to these matters is totally private and has no bearing on others, but it is not so with teachers and preachers. With them there are no victimless crimes: The what and the how of every communication are affected.

If this seems to be a call to the cloister, it only seems so. The task as Kierkegaard saw it was to have on him at all times the absolute demand while remaining in the relativities of life in the world. He compared it to the situation of diplomats who "acquire the self-control necessary to hold fast to the great plan, and at the same time make conversation with the ladies, dance, play billiards, and whatever else you like."[3] Teacher, preacher, theologian—all are under the burden constantly, not relieved of it by occasional successes in communicating the faith to others. "Let us not forget that in the schoolroom...it was the mediocre pupil who came running ten minutes after the task had been set, claiming to have finished."[4]

Of course, there are now and then those brilliant moments— clear, ecstatic, and successful—that, like Melchizedek, seem to be without father or mother. But Kierkegaard knew, and so do you and I, that in back of that flashing, effortless moment lie hours and days of uninspired study and work. I recall some years ago taking over a class for an ailing colleague. It was an Old Testament class, but he had the good grace to become ill far enough in advance to allow me to prepare. One hates to be a total fool, even when out of one's field. A night and a day I spent in deep concentration on the assignment, Psalm 91. Hebrew language, poetry, history, liturgy, and commentary were waded through in order to reach the podium. The students, having heard they were to endure a substitute, outstripped their own excellent record of nonpreparation. Of course, I growled, but privately I welcomed ignorance not only as unthreatening but as granting full release to my own recent wisdom. Against the dark background of their empty minds I cast the clear diamonds of critical analysis. For two hours the text was subjected to the best methods of biblical criticism. At the conclusion of the seminar we joined the entire seminary in the chapel to hold a memorial service for a respected teacher who had died suddenly of a heart attack. The worship leader read the text: Psalm 91. The appropriateness of the text was apparent: The text interpreted the occasion, and the occasion interpreted the text. Afterward, some of the students who had been in the seminar, in a mood of antiacademia, spoke to me in praise of the chapel service and in criticism of the apparent uselessness and sterility of our classroom exercise. In no way, they said, did our analysis of Psalm 91 compare with the immediacy and clarity of the reading in worship. There was truth to what they said; there is light on the page in the sanctuary that seldom comes in the classroom. Nevertheless, I reminded the students that we did not just hum the psalm in the chapel; we had attended to words, to a message from the psalmist for a particular occasion. We talked in the hallway at length about what that message was and listened to comments by students who were in chapel but not in the seminar. Before long, two observations were made: First, while all in the chapel were moved by the appropriateness of the text, probably none present quite grasped the meaning and power of Psalm 91 as did those who had carefully studied it; second, classroom and sanctuary should and do serve each other in the service of God.

In fact, should we not go further and say that study of the subject matter and work toward more effective communication of it are in a real sense worship? As rabbis have instructed their congregations, "an hour of study is, in the sight of the Holy One, Blessed be He, as an hour of prayer." And it is especially important that this be the governing consideration for those who teach and preach, those for whom the temptation to be performers in the sharing of their study is so great, especially for those who have ability at communicating. The only sure defense against the creeping absurdity that assumes that learning and expertise exempt the speaker from participating in the message so brilliantly urged upon others is to believe along with Kierkegaard: "The truth can neither be communicated nor be received except as it were under God's help, not without God's being involved as the middle term, He himself being the truth."[5]

This is not said simply to urge upon the teacher or preacher a way of life to support or reinforce what is said. Nor is it to endorse some particular exercise of introspection by which one indulges in trips through one's own psyche and calls it spirituality. Some postures of meditation may be little more than looking in myself, for myself, in order to aid myself.

> There was a certain man who moved into a cottage equipped with a stove and simple furnishings. As the sharp edge of winter cut across the landscape, the cottage grew cold, as did its occupant. He went out back and pulled a few boards off the house to kindle a fire. The fire was warm, but the house seemed as cold as before. More boards came off for a larger fire to warm the now even colder house, which in turn required an even larger fire, demanding more boards. In a few days the man cursed the weather, cursed the house, cursed the stove, and moved away.

What is being said really focuses not on forms of devotion before or after speaking, although these are certainly not foreign to the task of communicating, but rather on the posture of the communicator during the act of teaching or preaching. The most, if not only, appropriate posture for the speaker is that of worship. Regardless of the constituency of the class or congregation, the real audience is God. What we say or write, we offer to God. If I may get ahead of myself for a moment, it is not the case that God is overhearing what we say to those before us; it is rather the case that those before us are overhearing what we say to God. Is this not true? It must be, for how else can we remain faithful, how else pursue truth rather than expediency, how else be consistently Christian rather than depressed at failure and arrogant at success? When Kierkegaard wrote his reflections on his literary activity (*The Point of View for My Work as an Author*), he paused in the midst of those reactions to add an almost doxological note:

> Yet it delights me childishly that I have served in this way, whereas in relation to God I offer this whole activity of mine with more diffidence than a child when it gives as a present to the parents an object which the parents had presented to the child. Oh, but the parents surely are not so cruel that, instead of looking kindly upon the child and entering into its notion that this is a present, they take the

gift away from the child and say, "This is our property."
So it is also with God: He is not so cruel when one as a gift
brings to Him...His own.[6]

If all one's endeavor as teacher or preacher is conceived as an
offering to God, a sacrifice of the lips, then the posture appropriate
to that understanding is gratitude. Kierkegaard regarded it as a
common fault of the pulpit of his day that there was very much
standing on the legs and proving God's existence and very little
thanking God on the knees.

I have been urging participation in the life of faith and worship
as ingredient to communication lest one fall victim to the illusion
that participation is not necessary as long as one is a skilled
communicator. But if I do participate in what I say, a new problem
may arise—greater distance from the listeners. For if my work is
for and toward God, do I not have to fight the tendency to regard
people as intruders on this private (God and I) enterprise? If I
teach and preach in a sense on my knees, what are all these people
doing here? No one holds open house in a prayer room. The words
of every communication are very deeply my own, bathed in pathos
and joy, and an opportunity to share them publicly is at the same
time a temptation to remain silent or at least to speak of lesser
things. I can certainly identify with Somerset Maugham's feeling
about his plays. Even though he wrote for the theater, for the
public, still he confides,

> The fact is that, even in my lightest pieces, I had put in so
> much of myself that I was embarrassed to hear it disclosed
> to a crowd of people. Because they were words I had
> written myself they had for me an intimacy that shrank
> from sharing with all and sundry.[7]

And so, even on occasions when we are expected to speak,
there is an urge to withdraw into silence. Supported by the
conviction that the more public a matter the less depth, we are
tempted into elitism. Rather than sowing the seed on the rocky
soil and the good soil, on the path and in the weeds, we want to
select carefully each precise place and time for the Word. And all
the while there is that gnawing sense of guilt. Kierkegaard
struggled with this problem all his life. A man of extreme
introversion and very indecisive about taking specific steps in
any direction, he struggled in pain to be more open and

straightforward. Is this a problem only for those who spend a great deal of time in their own inner world, or does every serious speaker find at times the desire to be silent as strong or stronger than the desire to break the silence? Each of us must ask, "Am I so sensitive to the nuances of the gospel and to the feelings of my hearers that I wish to risk no pain to myself or anyone else, or am I a coward, fearing rejection and the loss of that sophistication that, secure in silence, could be lost any time I open my mouth?" I have, of course, just as some of you have, armed myself with those appropriate texts about not casting pearls before swine or that which is holy to the dogs. But my armor has also been stripped from me by God's instruction to shout from the housetop what was heard in a whisper.

This pain seems to come with the job. Kierkegaard tells a parable of a man who owned a magnificent jewel. It was most extraordinary, and he knew that it would get the praise of the public if he wore it. But he never wore it. He wanted to, but the occasion of sufficient importance never seemed to arise.[8] It seems easy enough to say to oneself, "Toss out the word; it will create its own audience; it will select its own listeners. Let him who has ears to hear, hear." But after all these years, that act remains for some of us, day after day, a most rigorous exercise of faith: a complete trust in the Word. And yet I cannot envy those who have created enough distance between themselves and the message so as to become easy talkers, free of pathos and the burden of listening to their own word and apparently oblivious to the contradiction in being what Kierkegaard calls "town criers of inwardness." The distance necessary for such performance may have been deliberately structured into the speaker's method under the illusion that professional excellence and longevity demanded it. Or the distance may have developed unconsciously as old habit took the place of conviction. The words and phrases are all there, and the appearance of teaching or preaching so approximates the real thing that the illusion is complete in its deception. And the speaker steps up to the platform as before, unaware as was Samson that he has been shorn of his strength, unable to name the day or hour when the glory of God departed.

There may be someone among you wondering why all this heavy sense of personal participation—after all, we preach not ourselves but Christ. Quite true. In fact, have we not all been nauseated by the speaker who "humbly boasted" that all he had to offer was his own experience, and then occupied us with his poorly disguised self-indulgence? Then why not toss aside the whole burden of self-involvement in the business of communication and clear the air by making a strategy of D. H. Lawrence's famous dictum: "Never trust the teller; trust the tale"?

The reasons are several. In the first place, Christian truth is simply not transmitted objectively as a thing, a statement, a piece of information, autonomous and unrelated to speaker and hearer. Christian communication is not just speaking truth. Kierkegaard has a story about a man who escaped from an insane asylum only to face the real prospect of being recognized as insane by the people in the nearest town and being returned to the institution. He decided to disguise his insanity by uttering aloud some generally accepted truth that would prove to all who heard him that he was sane. Finding a rubber ball in the street, he put it in the tail pocket of his coat where it bounced against his hind parts as he walked. With each bounce he said to any and all passersby, "The earth is round, the earth is round." Needless to say, he was recognized as insane and returned to the asylum. Why? Is it not the truth that the earth is round?[9] Yes, but the truth is not enough. There is something nonsensical about the truth in the mouth of one whose life has no evidence of participation in that truth. If your house cat looked up at you and asked, "When will we have dinner?" would you answer? It seems a reasonable question. It is with similarly ridiculous analogies that the philosopher Ludwig Wittgenstein taught us that the form of life out of which words come is inescapably involved in the meaning of the words. We do preach Christ and not ourselves, but the one who speaks the gospel does so from faith to faith, never in any sense exempt from its promise or judgment. The teacher or preacher does not thrill and move the hearers with a message on the uncertainties of life while proceeding on his or her own way certainly. The communicator is striving to become while urging others to become. To the extent that the speaker's struggle is everyone's, the listener can be brought thereby to clarity and to hope.

A second reason communication of the Christian faith cannot proceed when there is great distance between speaker and message is simply this: The act of communicating the gospel is in its very nature an act of passion. How else explain a person speaking before faces already bearing the rebuttal, "Who are you to be telling us?" Why else would anyone fly in the face of the popular notion that only those who have finished the race have anything to say to the runners? Is there any other way to understand a person's daily discipline of hard study wrapped in a prayer? The communicator is possessed by a profound passion. When this passion cools, when faith is no longer faith, then the communicator is, to use Kierkegaard's analogy, in the position of the young woman who finds she no longer loves her husband. Bound to him she no longer loves, she may now seek reasons in him for her attachment, qualities in him that she can describe to her friends and to herself as grounds for their relationship.[10]

Third and finally, Christian communication cannot tolerate the distance of nonparticipation between messenger and message because, to put it bluntly, that distance permits too much room for our own frailties to take over, our minds limping along behind, rationalizing and excusing behavior and attitudes that contradict our message. Against the background noise of the gradual erosion of the speaker's soul, the message is blurred and indistinct. I know as well as you do that the bird does not have to look like its song, but after we have found relief in the comfort of that thought, let us hear a ridiculous description by Kierkegaard:

> In the magnificent cathedral the Honorable and Right Reverend *Geheime-General-Ober-Hof-Pradikant*, the elect favorite of the fashionable world, appears before an elect company and preaches with emotion upon the text he himself elected: "God hath elected the base things of the world, and the things that are despised." And nobody laughs.[11]

Actually, it is very difficult to imagine anyone teaching, writing, or preaching the gospel without being altered thereby. Its power to transform is there, even though in each of us can be found some resistance to the gospel. But the truth is a snare. Kierkegaard watched the clever maneuvers of a mouse trying to get the cheese without being caught and reflected on the amusement of God over the clever moves of ministers.[12]

And so there is an *I* in the Christian message even though the subject is Jesus Christ. This is a fact, however much it may be disguised by the editorial *we* and obscured by vague generalizations about "modern man." If there is no *I*, there is no *Thou*, and the sermon or lecture is a thing dislodged, belonging to neither of us because it is not from me and it is not to you. It probably should be granted, however, that some may communicate impersonally, denying the *I* and the *Thou* from a sincere effort to avoid a common danger in teaching and preaching; namely, a hearer may become more interested in the messenger than in the message. And a speaker may discover that the result of her labor is not the stimulation of persons to appropriate the truth, but the formation of a circle of satellites. You probably have already remembered Kierkegaard's familiar story of the man who taught that no one should have disciples. So effective was he as a speaker that he received ten applications from persons wanting to be his disciples and share in the dissemination of his doctrine that no one should have disciples.[13]

The danger is real and constant, but surely the solution does not lie in maintaining cold distance from the listeners. On the contrary, here as in many situations, problems are best handled by moving nearer, not farther away. In fact, the notion that distance between speaker and hearer will prevent attachment to the messenger instead of the message is very likely the complete opposite of the truth. It is most often the distant, unapproachable, aloof, one who is made the sun for weak and admiring satellites. The relationship changes completely when the communicator moves toward the listeners, totally preoccupied with their experience of listening. The teacher or preacher who is consumed with the task of effecting a new hearing of the Word will be delivered from the fruitless questions of whether there is too much or too little distance or too much or too little involvement. To tackle the problem of effective communication by focusing on the speaker is about as effective as standing in front of a mirror wondering how to get one's mind off oneself. The difficulties of communicating in a context where the mood is low expectation and "more of the same" are so enormous that all concerns with authority, position, and public presence must be relinquished in the service of the hearing of the message. The difference between being a good speaker and effecting a hearing may at first seem slight to you, but two entirely different approaches to the task are involved. One can enjoy the wide reputation of being a good speaker and yet face the sad fact that hardly anyone has been altered thereby. This is no less true of the "good teacher."

If real success is to attend the effort to bring another person to a definite position, one must first of all take the pains to find that person where he or she is and begin there. This is the secret of the art of helping others. Anyone who has not mastered this is himself deluded when he proposes to help others. In order to help another effectively, I must understand more than he—yet first of all surely I must under-stand what he understands. If I do not know that, my greater understanding will be of no help to him. If, however, I am disposed to plume myself on my greater understanding, it is because I am vain or proud, so that at the bottom, instead of benefiting him, I want to be admired...To help does not mean to be a sovereign but a servant...not to be ambitious but to be patient.[14]

What Kierkegaard urges is no easy thing to do, putting oneself in the student's or listener's position. To understand what is understood and how it is understood means not only that you understand but that the listener understands that you do. This means, then, that the teacher or preacher will be willing to be subject to an examination by the listener; it means hearing from the listener what you may already know so that the listener may be sure you do. But that puts the teacher or preacher in the position of learning or seeming to learn from the learners. Can the ego take that?

Good gracious! This he could not venture to do, for fear the pupils might really believe that he did not understand it. That is to say, he is not fit to be a teacher, though he calls himself a teacher, he is so far from being such a thing that he actually aspires to be cited for commendation...by his pupils. Or as in the case of a preacher of repentance who, when he wants to chastise the vices of the age, is much concerned about what the age thinks of him.[15]

Now, frankly, I am having to wrestle with this a bit. I think of my students and my responses to occasional commendations from them. Why not welcome and savor them as a fringe benefit, especially on my slender salary? Of course, we all want and need strokes, but upon reflection, on what occasions did they come? This is the important question. Was it when I delivered the brilliant lecture, or was it when I was the learner and seemed to be a "no-teacher teacher" in order to effect their learning? And then there are my colleagues, and tenure, and all that! It is most difficult for the communicator to accept as a model the Incarnation, emptying oneself, making oneself of no reputation for the sake of others. The demanding point here is that it takes more than a Christian subject to have a Christian communication. Christ has given us the how as well as the what. I confess it is easier to try to master the what than to be mastered by the how.

It is instructive and humbling to see the unusual ways Kierkegaard made his own life contribute to his effort to get his message heard. In his literary activity, irony, humor, sarcasm, paradox, contradiction, personal experience, homely stories, gossip—all were his servants. Critics said he lacked dignity and seriousness. As Shakespeare used the fool to provide insight, as Faulkner used the idiot to present the profound, as the New Testament offers the truth from poor widow, beggar, and child, so Kierkegaard shaped himself into such contours as would make him a vessel to bear the message. In fact, Kierkegaard came to regard his own sickly and misshapen body—object of jokes and nicknames by children and which Kierkegaard often hated and wished to be rid of—as an aid in communicating the gospel. Ugliness, he said, keeps listeners from being only admirers and opens the ears to the message rather than the eyes to the messenger. He was nauseated by teachers of religion who described God in human form so perfectly proportioned and beautiful. Such a being would draw crowds without message or character or cause. Kierkegaard preferred to remember that Socrates was ugly, with clumsy feet and growths on his forehead, a condition that Socrates regarded as favorable to his work as a teacher, keeping the students engaged with the subject matter rather than with him.[16]

It was not his appearance alone, however, but his whole lifestyle that Kierkegaard regarded as an integral part of his work as a communicator. Conversations on the street, public appearances, presence or absence at social events—the rhythm of his daily routine was in concord with his writings so as to make the greatest impact. His behavior was a part of his overall method of communicating. I mention it not to offer his unusual lifestyle as a model but to prompt reflection on ways one's lifestyle can contribute to or can contradict one's attempts at communicating. Once a person is fully committed to sharing the Christian faith and every faculty of mind and heart has been released to that cause, the variety of possibilities in writing, speaking, and living are astounding. It is regrettable that for many of us, the style of our lives has not been included in the strategies of communicating, except rather limply in a moralistic sense: "Do not do anything that would weaken your message." Of course not, but how passive, defensive, and unimaginative! More regrettable, however, is that anxiety that locks in us all the rich possibilities for communicating, in word and act, and that makes us so harmlessly dull: the anxiety about what others may think of us. The ego, not voice or gestures, remains the teller's greatest obstacle in the path of effective communication of the story of faith.

"Something else is lacking, and this is a something which the one cannot directly communicate to the other." No doubt, a part of this "cannot" the teller shares with the listener, for the teller is quite often ineffective by reason of illusions about self and the relation of that self to the message and to the hearer. Before offering a proposal in response to the unrelenting question, How can one person communicate the Christian faith to another? I want us to look in one more corner for any remaining forms of illusion that haunt and hinder our task. We turn attention, then, away from teller and listener to the story itself.

4

Concerning the Story

There is no lack of information in a Christian land;
something else is lacking.

Again, Kierkegaard generates our conversation. The quotation above and countless other statements in Kierkegaard that point to the nonredemptive nature of information alone have been enough for critics of Kierkegaard to say that in his theology there is no such thing as *the* story; there is only *my* story. He has been accused of having no concern for Christian tradition or doctrine or scripture except as it lies experientially within the individual self. He has been charged with contracting all reality to those events and relationships that fall within the narrow parentheses of one's own birth and death. And there can be no denying that, as the father of existentialism, his writings have spawned frightening unconcern for history, for tradition, and for the life of the world, reviving the spiritualized self-interest of gnosticism and bringing about a subjective captivity of the church. The writings of Kierkegaard became the scholarly footnote legitimizing the transformation of theology into autobiography. Neither can it be denied that Kierkegaard did make strong comments (he never made any other kind) about the Christian enterprise, comments that on the lips of persons not in his context could be taken as dangerous disregard for the story, the subject matter of our faith. For example, he repeatedly insisted that "Christianity is not a doctrine but an existential communication."[1] In fact, he regarded the transmission of information as one of the lowest forms of communication. The highest form is the communication of the ability to feel obligated. Or again, "The very maximum of what one human being can do for another in relation to that wherein each man has to do solely with himself, is to inspire him with concern and unrest."[2]

I have no intention of trying to defend Kierkegaard, but a few words of clarification may help if he is to serve us in the formation of a method of communicating. Anyone who writes or speaks with the conviction that popular excesses need to be corrected will run the risk of being charged with partiality or heresy at the other extreme. Those without conviction or mission, those comfortably distant from the struggles of mind and heart that afflict the sincere, can sit on their patios and write symmetrical paragraphs on "both-and," giving equal space to each. But life is not symmetry; life is polemic, and we are here and not there, there and not here. There probably is a time when the need is not for someone with a burning idea but for an administrator of the ideas available, giving equal time and assuring a general democracy of thought. But Kierkegaard's was not such a time. It was not possible then and it is not possible now to be religious in general any more than it is to speak language in general. Kierkegaard knew this as well as any of us, and so he wrote and so he paid the price among those who read his works and rejected them as out of balance. But he was seeking not balance but a corrective to the church's offerings of predigested, homogenized doctrinal systems that intersected human life at no point. It was with clear-eyed intention that he sharpened an issue by exaggerations that were calculated to call forth a reaction. He entered a note in his Journal: "Dialectical as my nature is, it always looks as if the opposite thought were not present—but just then it comes forth strongest."[3] And again:

> He who must apply a "corrective" must study accurately and profoundly the weak side of the establishment, and then vigorously and one-sidedly present the opposite.

Precisely in this consists the corrective, and in this too the resignation of him who has to apply it. The corrective will in a sense be sacrificed to the established order. If this is true, a presumably clever pate can reprove the corrective for being one-sided. Ye gods! Nothing is easier for him who applies the corrective than to supply the other side; but it ceases to be the corrective and becomes the established order.[4]

And it is the task of those who follow not to repeat the corrective but to correct it. This method of teaching and otherwise communicating the Christian faith has so much to commend it to our circumstances that we must speak of it again. Our present effort is simply to take a moment to understand what Kierkegaard was doing by this method and, if it commends itself to us, to know the price to be paid for it. If others correct us, learning and understanding advance; if we are always careful to correct ourselves, our listeners become an audience hardly even amused by our little drama in which we play all the parts. Am I willing to be "corrected" for the advance of the gospel? Perhaps it will help our subsequent consideration of this method if we remind ourselves that it did not begin with Kierkegaard. Did not the prophets of Israel hurl words of correction against the idolatry of empty ritual and repetition, only to be accused of destroying sacred tradition? Did not Matthew seek to correct a kind of enthusiasm in the church that tended to disregard personal morality and social ethics, a corrective so near to legalism that many have wanted to correct his correction? Did not Paul and John use the category of the Holy Spirit to correct the tendencies of some to trap salvation in the shackles of past history, even though their correction brought charges of gnosticism?[5] But these and all correctives in the progress of the gospel are not to be understood as additions to the message to fill up what may be an inherent lack in the story. On the contrary, the correctives to excesses, like the excesses themselves, lie implicitly or explicitly within the story itself. Kierkegaard claimed no new proposals but rather called for reading once more the old original text handed down from the forebears, but in a more heartfelt way.

"The old original text handed down from the forebears"— they are wrong to say that for Kierkegaard there was only *my* story, not *the* story. And those who use classroom and sanctuary for exercises presuming to imitate Kierkegaard, but who lack Kierkegaard's context, are shadowboxing. To use a few excerpts from Kierkegaard as a permit to generate piety without the tradition is to generate mutations bearing only slight resemblance to Abraham's race. Placing one's finger on one's own pulse is not doing theology. There is the story, and Kierkegaard would have agreed with Theodor Adorno: "Forgetting is inhuman." Of course, Kierkegaard concentrated on the subjective world, because his concern was for the modes of human existence. Of course, Kierkegaard concentrated on the subjective world, because the church seemed to have forgotten that there is subjectivity in the very nature of the Christian faith in that it deals not just with events and ideas but also with interests, passions, confessions, convictions, and value judgments. But he would be the first to acknowledge that the Christian revelation centers not in ourselves, not in some recollection of a preexistent state as with Plato, not in some ancestral deposit in the collective unconscious of the race as with Jung, but in the Incarnation. It could not be stated more clearly than in Kierkegaard's own discussion, *On Authority and Revelation*:

> Christianity exists before any *Christian* exists, it must exist in order that one may become a Christian, it contains the determinant by which one may test whether one has become a Christian, it maintains its objective subsistence apart from all believers, while at the same time it is the inwardness of the believer...Though Christianity comes into the heart of ever so many believers, every believer is conscious that it has not arisen in his heart, is conscious that the objective determinant of Christianity is not a reminiscence.[6]

I have taken time to say these things out of a concern that is methodological, to understand *how* Kierkegaard communicated, a concern that has at its root the conviction that inasmuch as our circumstances are not totally dissimilar, he can instruct us. But if we do not properly appreciate what he sought to do in his context, then we shall learn amiss. It is when we are aware of what he could assume as the Christian conditioning of his readers that we appreciate his methods. I offer the spice, not the meal, he said; I feed people by taking food out of the mouths of those whose mouths are too full, he said; I function as a smoke-consumer, he said, so that the room will be cleared.

If, then, we have persuaded ourselves that there is in the chemistry of the work of Kierkegaard, and of ourselves, not just the speaker and the listener but also the story, let us return to the question: Are there difficulties in communicating that lie not in the speaker or listener but in the story itself? We tiptoe here because we both know we are talking about the Bible. In approaching the Bible, the twin essentials for good communication, distance and participation, meet us immediately and unavoidably. The distance between the text and the reader is too obvious to miss: strange language, remote places, unfamiliar names, ancient times. This distance poses a major problem for any serious reader, but it is at the same time a blessing, for the distance preserves the integrity of the Christian faith against any tendency to sacrifice and consume the past by any reader insisting on an immediate and relevant word at this moment. On the other hand, participation is also intrinsic to the nature of the Bible; this is what it means to call it the church's scripture, the living Word as the norm for faith and life. And yet we all know how, in the absence of distance, this participation in the text by the reader can sink into anti-intellectual, visceral exercises, not hearing *the* story, but confirming and comforting *my* story. With distance and participation so clearly present as both promise and threat to the communication of the Christian faith, it will be apparent in all that follows how the Bible contributes to and at the same time fights against illusions and distortions in the preaching and teaching of the church.

There is no evidence that Kierkegaard saw in the Bible itself any obstacles to communicating the Christian faith. On the contrary, direct exposure to the text could well serve to break the shackles put on the gospel by clerics and professors. He recognized and respected the work of critical scholars within the province of their own proper aims and with the understanding that biblical criticism alone could not generate faith or make anyone happy. Kierkegaard felt that the amount of interpretation of the Bible had become so massive that it was a hindrance to understanding, much as too many spotlights prevent rather than aid one's seeing a play. In Protestantism especially, he said, "Emphasis on the Bible has brought forth a religiosity of learning and legal chicanery, sheer diversion. A kind of knowledge of this sort has gradually trickled down to the simplest people so that no one can read the Bible humanly any more."[7] But Kierkegaard is not falling into the hands of the anti-intellectuals who regard serious study as a threat to immediate appropriation. The immediacy with which the reader participated in the message of scripture was always for him an immediacy that came after disciplined investigation and reflection. His charge was that the clergy and the professors did not trust the word of scripture, but were constantly building around it the scaffolding of eighteen centuries of dogma, tradition, ecclesiastical machinery, and claims of authority. Whenever he had opportunity to preach, invariably it was an occasion for sharing the promise and judgment of a text of scripture. Quite unlike the sermons and lectures of the church, the Bible for Kierkegaard had the quality of a conversation, between God and God's people.

What Kierkegaard is saying is so central to my own thought and so quickening to my imagination that I wish to say Amen and move on. No doubt, power and therapy would come to pulpit, pew, and classroom by such exercises, but in our context, and most likely in Kierkegaard's, certain unavoidable facts soon discipline and instruct movements back to the Bible. The distance is not easily negotiated. For example, any return to the Bible, any attack on distance, must face up to the fact that such return does not take us back prior to Easter, to a time when faith had to gather its reasons from the life and suffering and death of Jesus of Nazareth. In fact, such a return does not even take us back to a time when the Bible was not the "canon," the authoritative norm for life and faith. For the believing community, the anecdotal and conversational character of much of the Bible is now "Holy Writ." Jesus paused to speak to a wayside beggar. Those words are now in red letters and are read everywhere by sober brows as texts giving authority to lesson and sermon. Jesus elevated life as the stuff of revelation, but now the everyday stuff rests on a draped table between white candles. Jesus told parabolic stories that interested listeners by their casual and common themes and that captured listeners by their open-ended wait for response. Now those stones are sacred scripture, and a canonical, authoritative, inspired, and divine parable is hardly any longer just a parable. The *invitation* to listen is gone; I *must* listen to the story, as well as to its explanations and applications, both within and without the text itself. It seems a negative effect of canonization that discovery is no longer a posture of faith, that the listener to these stories and sayings no longer ascertains if there is in them the word of God. It is as the experience of a visitor to Israel who, fully intent on discovery, is on arrival forced to experience "the Holy Land"; there are no discoveries, only melted candles and shrines. The whispered paradox of Bethlehem has become a shout.

Do not misunderstand; no attacks open or subtle on the canon are being entertained. I shudder to think at whose shrine I would be kneeling without it. The issue before us has to do with communication. You and I are intent on creating a new hearing of the Word among those who have heard it countless times before. We do it by telling the old story. But if we recite it as it is written, listeners say, "Here we go again." On the other hand, try some imaginative new perspective, and the church board wants an explanation for flippant and irreverent treatment of Holy Scripture. And they may have a point.

We might as well face it—some of the difficulty of communicating lies within the story itself. Lively metaphors once quickening mind and heart to new visions of reality are now, through long use, flat and commonplace. "The language of the New Testament has become so familiar it has lost its edge."[8]

Robert Funk wrote a book entitled *Jesus as Precursor*. The unusual nature of the book flows from the author's desire that his readers have a discovery, a "for the first time" experience in the parables of Jesus. Whatever his success, Professor Funk has addressed himself to the immense task that faces us here.

> Because it [the biblical corpus] has suffered over-attention, its language has been overlaid with tons of obfuscating debris. To change the metaphor, few literary compendia in the Western tradition have been so completely washed clean of resonances by the waters of common repetition and interpretation. Is it possible to restore some of those resonances or cart away some of that debris? If so, what is the appropriate critical methodology?
>
> One thing may be stipulated by way of anticipation: the methodology must be appropriate to the subject matter.[9]

As you probably have already anticipated, the methods we use are extremely important, because they not only are to be appropriate to the subject matter, but methods tend to give their own character to the subject matter. The way I approach and share the Bible tends to define what the Bible is, for me and eventually for the listeners. Much of the difficulty we face in effecting a new hearing of the Word lies, therefore, in the methods we have used.

This is true in some cases simply because the methods are not appropriate to the subject matter. This is true in other cases not because the methods are inappropriate, but because the methods, including their positive results, are a part of the "common repetition and interpretation" that has rendered us deaf and blind to the story. Let us think for a few minutes about how the story has been handled, hopeful that the gains and losses of biblical study will help us chart the course before us.

Perhaps the way to begin is with a confession that all of us are guilty of having participated in violations against the story even while sincerely hoping to keep distance and participation in creative tension. What has been, through all our misuses of the story, the most common methodological error? E. D. Hirsch has described the act of interpretation in terms of two moments: intuition (the discovery, the insight, the vision) and precision (the careful weighing of the intuition).[10] It would be most satisfying to claim both moments as usual preparation for teaching and preaching; to claim one would at least save some embarrassment. But quite often preparation proceeds on a principle that does not qualify as a "moment" at all; more honestly it should be called utilitarianism. Regrettably, teaching and preaching in the church are seldom seen as producing, contributing to the continuation of the discourse we call "the story," but more often as consuming, using parts of the story already easily available for a sermon or lesson.

Take, for example, the expression "biblical preaching." It is commonly understood as referring to uses of biblical materials in a substantive way in preaching. But think for a moment of the expression as meaning "how the Bible preaches." Such a perspective might at least have the value of delaying our pursuit of a lecture or sermon long enough to see how the Bible itself does it. After all, distance and participation are not just factors we bring to the Bible; the Bible itself had to deal with them in its effort to keep telling its own story.

How does the Bible communicate? We could, of course, respond with a list: stories, songs, liturgies, biographies, historical narrative, legends, parables, proverbs, and so on. That alone could be instructive and perhaps refresh our own patterns of communication. But several general characteristics might be kept in mind if our own methods are framed so as not to violate the integrity of the story but rather to be, as Professor Funk says, "appropriate to the subject matter."

In the first place, the Bible addresses the community of faith and is not a collection of theological and ethical arguments to persuade atheists or adherents of other religions. As James Barr has reminded us, "What you learn about God is not the first contact with deity; it is new information about a person whom you already know."[11] The church has a long history of using the Bible to prove the existence of God and a history almost as long of using the Bible to legislate for society as a whole the convictions of the Christian community. I do not wish here to argue for or against the merits of such uses, although you probably sense my drift away from these exercises. Both distance and appropriation are violated by such arbitrary applications. All I wish to say now is that this characteristic of the Bible, along with its assumptions about the people to whom it addresses itself, should be a part of those methods of sharing the story that we employ.

Second, it is generally characteristic of the Bible not to repeat a story verbatim and from that story draw lessons and exhortations appropriate to the particular audience, but rather to retell the story in such a way that it properly addresses the hearers. Stories of Abraham, of the exodus, of Moses, of David, of Jesus—all are told, retold, and then told again. And why? If these are the stories of the community, and if the community has continuing life before God, and if the stories are vehicles of God's revelation, why not? Contact with the original is not lost, but neither are the new listeners disregarded as though they were not involved in the story. But many are not content to let the Bible retell stories for new auditors. A preferred goal of some seems to be to count the times a narration occurs with little variation and to hurl that statistic into the face of those who doubt the historical accuracy of the record. If that is the way to use the Bible, then Matthew and Luke and especially John render such an interpreter a disservice by their "alterations" of the story as we have it in the earlier Mark. But when pressed, blame can always be put on some weak-eyed copyist with flickering candle. And if hard pressed, there is always the analogy of four witnesses to an accident describing it four ways. How I hate that analogy! It not only assumes that the quality sought by the writer was precision (not to be discounted altogether, of course), but it also attributes the differences in the stories to human frailty rather than to the ancient and powerful art of addressing the particular needs of those before you by retelling old stories. The Bible interprets itself productively, not reproductively.

The dangers inherent in such cycling and recycling of narratives are obvious. When is continuity with the original so broken that the community is derailed and identity obscured? The question has to be asked continually, but there is no better guide than the Bible itself. For example, Luke records a parable of Jesus concerning a feast and guests who did not come. Matthew tells the story for his situation, and it is now an allegory with historical allusions. The gospel of Thomas tells it for another situation as a morality story against the business community. There is no need for us to mutter about poor memory or lack of appreciation for a parable; the writers are carrying out the obligation to bring the word of Jesus in the tradition to bear upon the lives of their readers. If as interpreter, teacher, and preacher, I am to continue that discourse here and now—it is frightening. But there is comfort and correction in the knowledge that my retelling the story is done in a community that carries the tradition and listens to me through its memory. Without the continuing community of faith, the isolated and private interpretations of preachers and teachers would likely erase the trail of the tradition, and we would lose our way.

Third, it is quite characteristic of the Bible to address particular situations and not worry about harmonizing each message with all its other messages on that topic.

The Old Testament can tolerate vigorous opposition to kingship as well as proud proclamations of the coronation of the king as God's "Son." It can share the broad sympathies of the stories of Ruth and Jonah but also the solid nationalism of Haggai and Malachi. The New Testament can urge one group to become as little children and another to quit being children without feeling it must harmonize the two into one harmless and helpless exhortation. Jesus can command one candidate for discipleship to leave all other responsibilities immediately and instruct another to sit down and first count the cost. The Bible speaks to particular human situations and does not have homogenized treatments of themes of biblical theology: Kingdom, Salvation, Messianism, Covenant, Sin, Atonement, Eschaton. Neither does it have simple plans of salvation for witnesses in a hurry: The Four Steps to Heaven, or The Eight Rungs of the Ladder to Glory, each item well stocked with verses gleaned from all sixty-six books. It often happens that a preacher will take a proper text to address his listeners, a text sharp and on target, but being anxious to assure the hearers that he knows there are other passages that approach the matter differently, he fills the air with such a balanced range of perspectives that the congregation escapes untouched somewhere between "on the one hand" and "but on the other hand." It sometimes happens that a teacher will exercise such caution in giving various views equal time that the students pass the course but do not find any view worth buying since everything seems to be on sale.

As we have already noted briefly, Kierkegaard recaptured beautifully this characteristic of the Bible to make one point at a time, with no anxiety about harmony, balance, and symmetry. There is a time and place for organization of ideas into conceptual systems, but that is later. First comes the edge of one disturbing word. Without that, all is rote and serves only to buttress the illusion that the truth has been spoken and heard. Kierkegaard had no patience with preachers who, instead of presenting Christianity as infinitely severe and as infinitely lenient, offered a severity weakened by leniency and a leniency weakened by severity. No one had any trouble digesting these small dishes of soft grace. Anybody can do it; all it involves is taking several solid texts of scripture, pausing to remind oneself to protect the Bible and the people from each other with the principle "There are no contradictions in the Bible," and then carefully straining the texts through the fine meshes of one's theological system. The good folk will not even have to chew.

Finally, it is generally characteristic of the Bible to present its message in vivid images, analogies, and metaphors. It is to Kierkegaard's credit that he refused to abandon these in his writing. He not only preserved them, but the biblical imagery stirred him to think and write vividly so that the reader could apprehend through eye and ear and mouth and nose and finger. He knew, of course, the price one pays for this: Detractors find it interesting or amusing but lacking in sophistication and academic dignity. Have you ever sat on a Sunday morning before a reading of some rich text, moved by the ancient imagery: hills skipping as lambs, the earth shaking under the heavy foot of the Almighty walking up to Jerusalem from Sinai, God with a long white beard, a valley of dry bones, a tender sprout on an old stump, Satan plaguing the solitude of Jesus in the fierce desert, Paul caught up to the third heaven, streets of gold and a chorus of white robed saints? Soon kindred images—some sober, some foolish—are spawned in the listener's stirred mind. Then the preacher arises to "explain" all the images to the "modern mind." What is offered is really a disguised apology for the poor ancient writer. Why do I as a listener have to choose between a naive embrace of the biblical imagery and a lifeless product of scholarly excavations in the text? I resist the nonacademic or anti-intellectual, but something is wrong. What is it?

It may be that we are guilty of an intellectual distortion of the faith. Amos Wilder is surely on target when he describes the difference between our efforts to deal with life at the level of ideas and those of biblical writers who knew "not only how to clarify ideas but to give signals that could awake a deep resonance in the hearts of men."[12] Perhaps the imagery of the Bible, shocking as some of it is, more accurately portrays the nature of humanity and history than do those more recent diagrams of illness and healing within the self. As we shall discuss later, biblical studies are suffering from a lack of imagination, but there are signs of a new realization that what the scripture communicates "is to be grasped by the same kind of imaginative apprehension that first shaped it, and only then transposed provisionally into conceptual statement."[13] Hopefully we are recovering somewhat from the past century as described by Paul Holmer: "Everyone seems to have forgotten, in the enthusiasm for finding the myths and superstitions, bad metaphysics and pre-scientific cosmology that were probably contemporaneous, the fear of the Lord, the contriteness of spirit, the broken hearts, the pathos and need that were also there."[14]

We have by these last comments moved away from the more common use of the Bible in the church classroom and pulpit and into the realm of critical scholarship. The one is an exercise in participation, the other in objective distance. These should not be two entirely different tasks, but the two enterprises are distinct enough that for purposes of discussion we will consider them separately. We turn, then, to comment briefly on ways in which roadblocks in the path of communicating the Word are constructed by biblical scholarship.

What has happened in the history of biblical scholarship, a discipline unquestionably motivated by the desire to recover and understand the ancient text, that would lay it open to any charge of hindering the communication of that text? At the risk of radical reduction and oversimplification, three observations will be made.

First, biblical criticism was gradually moved out of the department of humanities, where it was born, and isolated to become an intramural exercise. Even when it is granted that some degree of isolation is essential for intense scholarly endeavor, just think of what was lost in the move. The pioneers in biblical criticism were men of broad education and sympathies, familiar with great literature and at home in all the humanities. They treated biblical literature with literary respect and wrote their scholarly reports with literary skill. It takes an artist to treat properly the artistry of a prophetic oracle. Canons for evaluation were drawn not just from history and science but from literature. The form of a biblical passage was not shunted aside as a decorative incidental.

But it is not so now. Find a book in the field of biblical studies that is in itself good literature, and its scholarship is questioned. So predominant have become the concerns for facticity and historicity that any aesthetic appreciation of the Bible is immediately regarded as a device for avoiding the subject matter. Study of the Bible as a body of literature came to be regarded as the paltry business of the liberals who, we were warned, do not really believe the Bible, so they treat it along with Milton and Shakespeare. And, of course, in tax-supported schools they have to play those literary games, and the true believers permit it as rather harmless. In seminaries and churches, however, we deal with the "real stuff." You may recall that when an English translation of the Bible appeared some years ago with the poetic passages appearing in poetic form, there was strong suspicion in some quarters that the translators saw the Bible as great literature and therefore not the word of God. I do not overstate the case: The story of the separation of biblical studies from the humanities reads like a tragedy.

Second, in the wake of this separation, another separation occurred. With biblical studies moved away from the lively presence of interest in form, style, and art that characterized the department in which critical study of the Bible was born, it was not long until there occurred the divorce between form and content. And if in divorce suits charges must be brought as grounds for the action, then *content* accused *form* of being incidental, accessory, not substantive, and often only decorative. *What* claimed to be able to live purely and freely apart from *how*. Recall, for example, the history of parable interpretation beginning with

Adolph Jülicher, who is regarded as the father of modern study of parables. Jülicher operated on the principle that the interpreter's task is to get the substantive point conveyed by the parable, which was merely its literary vehicle. Once the point, the content, the information, was gotten, the parable as form was dispensable. Subsequently, those other two masters of parable investigations, C. H. Dodd and Joachim Jeremias, kept the same operating principle, disagreeing solely on what the point of a particular parable was, based on their own further historical (not literary) investigations. Not until very recently, as we shall discuss soon, has there been any departure from Jülicher.

What prevailed in parable interpretation was generally the state of affairs in all investigations of biblical texts and, with few exceptions, remains so today. Even literary criticism has served only as a handmaiden of content, running errands for the historian. The operating principle: There is in the text a body of knowledge or information, having existence apart from and therefore extractable from the literary forms. Words in all their various arrangements are treated as having one function—reference to the content. Biblical criticism struggled long and hard to establish itself as a science respected by other sciences for its methods and results. That it succeeded was not an unambiguous victory.

> As far as science is concerned language is simply an instrument, which it profits it to make as transparent and neutral as possible. It is subordinate to the matter of science (workings, hypotheses, results) which, so it is said, exists outside language and precedes it. On the one hand and first there is the content of the scientific message, which is everything; on the other hand and next, the verbal form responsible for expressing that content, which is nothing.[15]

The third and final observation concerning the way in which biblical criticism has shaped itself into an obstacle to the communication of the very story with which it works follows naturally the second: The content that preoccupied biblical scholarship was history. Accepting the formula that "what actually happened" equals truth and reality, the canons of historical research were applied to the biblical records and became the overruling method in the field. The history of the ancient Near East was being reconstructed, and the Bible fit, partially fit, or did not fit into that total picture. The definition of the Bible as history and the priority put on facticity as *the* value controlled the enterprise. Motives, of course, differed. Some saw themselves working as objective historians, establishing the biblical department as a reputable discipline in the university. Others overtly or covertly sought to demonstrate the nonhistorical character of much of the Bible, thinking thereby to break the dogma and authority of an obsolete church. Still others sought as diligently to prove the historicity of the acts and events chronicled in scripture, assuming that positive results would authenticate and legitimate faith. Giants of biblical scholarship rose to the task, people who would have been a credit to any field of research. Monumental additions to the sum of human knowledge were produced. Such gains were made in what we know about the Bible that some prescientific fallacies in biblical studies can never be repeated. But we are talking about communicating the Word, and from that perspective, some tragic results fall as shadows across this grand endeavor. That distance without participation equals truth was and is an illusion.

Consider, for instance, the impact of this preoccupation with history on the church's understanding of what the Bible is. That the scriptures are inspired the church has always claimed, but what does that mean? "All scripture is inspired by God and is useful for teaching," states Second Timothy, urging the usefulness of the ancient texts for teaching and discipline in the faith. From this passage one could argue that the accent on inspiration has more to do with getting the Word *off* the page than *on* it, more to do with the Spirit's work in keeping the past words present, active, and functioning in the community. But now inspiration has increasingly come to refer to the Spirit's work in getting the words *on* the page, written accurately, errorlessly, recording precisely the facts as to what was said and done. The development of printing and the associated legalities of authorship, copyrights, and the fixity of words on pages all work to support this line of thought. Even today, ask members of the church what *inspiration* means, and most answers will deal with accurate reporting. So predominant is this notion that it is assumed to be *the* true and biblical definition. Those having a different perspective on the nature and function of scripture are often made to feel they are abandoning "the doctrine of inspiration."

The stress on historicity inevitably led also to heavy gravitation toward the historical portions of the Bible. Poetic, proverbial, and dramatic materials suffered from mass neglect, except, of course, as they were involved in the historical questions of authorship and date. What else about a poem could interest the historian? And with "style"—that quality of writing that can involve, evoke, and engage the reader meaningfully—now totally peripheral to the central discussion of content, who would dare suggest any connection between inspiration and literary artistry? The deadly effects on "Bible teaching" and "Bible preaching," whether by literalist or liberal, were criminal. Imagine one person tossing out Shakespeare's *Othello* because there is no historical evidence that there ever was a Moorish general in the service of Venice, while another person embraces it as "true" because a rare footnote in an ancient history of Italy proved a Moor once so served.

Is this to disregard the importance of history? By no means! Only a fool or a person living in a private subjective world would be so inclined. But the viselike grip of historicism has to be broken, or the sacred text will be forced to answer questions it is not designed to answer, and, more importantly, it will not be allowed to do its full work of moving across the wide range of human faculties of mind, heart, and will, stirring, confirming, disturbing, renewing. We are to live *fully*, not just *accurately*, whatever that is. The Bible carries the power of a full literary spectrum: history, biography, poem, prayer, vision, parable, proverb, correspondence, oracle, sermon. How dare anyone diminish that with some grim exercise in which the magnet of facticity is passed over it, gathering the "true" and leaving the remainder marked with a tag that condescendingly explains, "Of course, we know today that..."

You see, what has happened is that under the rubric of historical criticism the tradition has been turned into history. The tradition is a narrative, an ingenious mingling of history and nonhistory, experience and interpretation, into a continuous story. Because that story is alive, modifying and being modified by the terrain of generations through which it passes, including the present, then it is my story. History, on the other hand, *was*; it happened and has been recorded, and hence is not my story but theirs. Only by a diligent hermeneutical endeavor can it be brought into my world. In the tradition narrative we are participants in the sequence, not independent observers. A tradition renders its meaning and power to the community and to its individual members by the very process of narration, which is indispensable to the tradition. The narration is so significant to the life and identity of the community that its being read or told was a sacred act contexted by introits, prayers, and songs. But historical criticism, fearing the loss of objectivity through such involvement in the material, by its methods moved the text further from readers and listeners. Preserve distance, it said; participation blurs one's vision.

It takes little imagination to see what problems of interpretation were created by this new distance. Greater bifurcation occurred between what a text *meant* and what a text *means*.[16] Some scholars began to refer to the task of getting at what a text meant as exegesis and at what a text means as hermeneutics, but the movement from the one to the other was not smooth. Why? With what Hans Frei has called "the eclipse of biblical narrative," the continuity of the narrated tradition has been broken into *their* world and *our* world. Historical research has left clearly the *impression* that what is central, perhaps we could even say normative or canonical, is not the text but the actual events back of them to which the text refers. Under this pressure, the Bible is less scripture in the sense of having a present Word and more an ancient book that reports—sometimes accurately, sometimes inaccurately—some events in the history of the Near East. We have learned during this time immeasurably more than we ever knew about the Bible, but regrettably, as Kierkegaard would say, no one was made happy. "There is no lack of information in a Christian land; something else is lacking."

It was and is inevitable that reactions began that sought to overcome the distance of history and provide the something that is lacking. When the text ceases to be a story mediating revelation and meaning, the reaction is to dismiss the past and "sink into the warm stream of the immediate."[17] If historical criticism broke the sense of narrative time by abstraction from the present, the reactions broke it by contraction into the present only. These approaches also lost the narrative, even though some seemed to have been momentarily refreshed by the authority of the immediate and spontaneous. In churches and seminaries we treated one another to biblical texts that launched "gut level," "but how do you feel?" "now is where it is" discussions of life. An exciting shift, to be sure, but without the parent story, an orphan is still an orphan.

Fortunately, however, there have been less reactionary and more responsible efforts to recover the loss of narrative that the Bible, and hence its readers, suffered under the predominating influence of historicism. A most hopeful direction in biblical studies in recent times has occurred through an effort to renew the ancient tie between biblical criticism and literary criticism. Literary paradigms had long ago been abandoned for historical paradigms in the study of scripture. But Bible scholars are again saying that the Bible is, after all, literature. Whatever the sources and historical origins of Genesis or the gospel of Mark, we must not overlook the fact that these come to us as pieces of literature in which form and content are wedded so as to create certain effects on the reader. There has been a return to Aristotle's poetics and not just his rhetoric. Literary criticism, long the servant of historical criticism, has taken on new life as a genuine investigation of the literary forms and communicative skills of biblical materials. For example, William Beardslee and Robert Tannehill have both written recently exploring how proverbial intensification, parabolic exaggeration, chronological narration, and other literary structures function to effect changes in a reader or hearer of the New Testament. The broad basic rediscovery has been in seeing anew the powers of language other than the power of simply conveying information.[18]

The most fruitful work in this new alliance with literary criticism has been done in parable interpretation. The parable is the example par excellence of a piece of literature that is not designed to convey information, but by its very form arrests the attention, draws the listener into personal involvement, and leaves the final resolution of the issue to the hearer's own judgment. The force of the parable lies in the metaphor that is "nothing other than the application of a familiar label to a new object which first resists and then surrenders to its application."[19] Set the metaphor with its power to create a new perspective (for example, street bums at the king's table) within a brief story with its power to hold attention, and the result, a parable, is a classic demonstration of the irreducible quality of form as ingredient to the power of the word of scripture. The Bible and its honest transmission in lesson and sermon can never be content to submit solely to questions of facts and information. Nothing could be more unbiblical, not to mention uninteresting and ineffective.

But enough of this. Our minds have already been led around another corner. Kierkegaard was certainly right: There is no lack of information, but something else is lacking. The stone the builders rejected was the hearer. Encouragingly, quite a few current biblical scholars have become interested in communication, in reaching the listener, and not as a second field of scholarship. If to call the Bible scripture means that the text has not just a past but a future, and that future is toward the reader/listener, then communication is a necessary dimension of biblical study. Before the world, inner and outer, of the hearer, most biblical scholars stand, drawn and challenged by the territory unexplored. Here again, Kierkegaard will help us. He is unparalleled as an explorer into the realm of the hearer, and his maps of that terrain are guides to our reaching it through speaking and writing.

Part II

*An Attack upon
the Illusion*

5

By Way of Kierkegaard

There is no lack of information in a Christian land;
something else is lacking, and this is a something which the
one cannot directly communicate to the other.

We proceed toward a proposal for a mode of communicating that is aware of the difficulties we have been discussing. I say *aware of* the difficulties because while we hope that the proposal will overcome some of the problems, all who communicate know that some difficulties lie irremovably in the task. In fact, it might even be the case that some difficulties, by sustaining tension, function creatively to keep the "in process" character of the transaction. But about such a proposal let me express both a conviction and an observation.

First, the conviction: Whether we teach or preach or both, we have no more urgent or important or demanding task than that of effecting a new hearing of the gospel. Communication is not a second and optional field subordinate to Bible or theology or church history or parish administration. Christianity, whether in broad perspective or in narrow assignment, is communication.

To say "new" hearing is not to offer a judgment on earlier hearings but to emphasize that the gospel is to be heard ever anew, a condition made most difficult by its having been heard before. To meet that challenge taxes all the faculties of thought and imagination. Kierkegaard insisted, "The distinguishing characteristic in life is not what is said but how it is said."[1] And to say "hearing" is to focus attention where it belongs: on the listener's experience. It is not helpful to insist we want to be better communicators; that introduces a checklist of qualities that pertain to the speaker and draws attention away from the purpose of the activity: that someone hear. We might as well confess it: The ego of the teacher or preacher very often prevents the necessary concentration on the listener. For the listener the speaker gives up claims, authority, public esteem, appearance, notions of advancement. Refuse that sacrifice, and one's career is marked by the frantic search for that good book on teaching or preaching, or better yet, that helpful cassette tape that I can play in the car, sharpening my skills while I drive.

Second, along with this conviction concerning the need to effect a new hearing among those already overexposed and dulled by repetition is this accompanying observation: To achieve this is extremely difficult. Part of the difficulty lies, as has been said, in a misdirection among teachers and preachers who are occupied with what they are to say and neglect the complex dynamics of communicating. But a major hurdle consists of the tendency among us to resist change in our style. "Every honest man has to confess that in a very short time even the most honest of men becomes enamored with his own method if he is not constrained to expose himself to a completely different light."[2] Vocabulary and language become stereotyped in meanings conveyed, and lose connotative depth. Through long and repeated use, methods once helpful now aggravate the condition they were designed to cure. Kierkegaard spoke often of the danger of his own accents and methods, if given too long a life or if copied by others, producing results the opposite of his intention. Others have agreed: "To make the language of faith of a given period, even that of the New Testament, absolute would be to deny that Jesus is Lord of all history, including our own."[3] But let us not think we have here a vocabulary problem to be handled by sprinkling our lectures and sermons with current jargon. The problem is a much bigger one: poor timing, frozen imagination, insecurity, self-consciousness, lack of empathy, and a general unwillingness to lose oneself in the task of communicating.

In short, we are talking about being *appropriate,* appropriate in language, mood, and style to the message, the listeners, the occasion. I surprise myself with the weight of importance I now put on fittingness. It was not always so. Appropriate has to do with what is proper, and in the vigorous enthusiasm of my camel hair and leather girdle days I saw absolutely no kinship between the weighty matters of the faith and concern for what is proper. Our religion is made of sterner stuff: Speak of right or wrong, good or evil, true or false, but not of proper or improper as though our business were to lecture on good manners. But through the intervening years, I have observed the inappropriate. At times it has been comical, as Mary's lamb at school. At other times, painful, as Prince Hamlet felt the inappropriateness of his mother's marriage to his uncle before the flowers had faded on his father's grave. And on occasion, the fragile phrase "out of place" has defined evil. Is not a drug quite often a medicine out of place? Is not Satan an angel out of place? On the other hand, all of us have known the beauty and power and goodness of the appropriate word or card or act or gift. There is unmatched eloquence in the appropriate word. Of course, we do not forget true and false, but when Jesus clashed with the Pharisees over fasting, it was not truth but appropriateness that was at issue. The story of the prodigal son raises sharply a question concerning the kingdom: Is it appropriate to throw a party for a prodigal? One could go so far as to say that the word of God is that revelation which fits the occasion, which is appropriate.

No one felt the painful comedy of travesties against appropriate time and place and style more than Kierkegaard. He entered a sad note in his journal about a man telling very close friends of his wife's death with the words, "Burial will take place from St. Peter's Church, notice of which is hereby announced." It reminded Kierkegaard of the style of many bloodless sermons.[4] On another occasion he reflected on how profoundly fitting were the words "We shall meet again" on a tombstone. However, put those same words on the lips of an acquaintance you chance to meet on a busy street, and they seem foolish.[5]

Upon this observation about method, then, and upon the conviction that makes it more than casually interesting, we move to a proposal about communicating. Our movement may seem to you a bit circuitous since we are going by way of Kierkegaard, but I am sure that listening to him will add not only interest to the trip but substance to the proposal. In fact, a major fear is that you will be loathe to leave the delights of Kierkegaard's brilliant insights to enter the plateau of my own subsequent offering. A minor fear is that his comments will be so full of prophecy that you will arrive early and on your own at my suggestion and find my paragraphs unnecessary. No, on the contrary, I would be pleased at such a consummation, your independent experience tending to confirm the value and appropriateness of my conclusions. We will, then, briefly explore Kierkegaard's method of communicating, not out of historical interest, but convinced that it provides raw material for a style by which our own effectiveness may be increased.

Kierkegaard operated with and often discussed two styles of communication: direct and indirect. He regarded direct as the mode for transferring information and considered it totally appropriate to the fields of history, science, and related disciplines. The indirect was the mode for eliciting capability and action from within the listener, a transaction that did not occur by giving the hearer some information. Kierkegaard was very sensitive to the nuances of these two forms, especially as they affected the listener. He regarded some methods used by preachers and teachers as totally disrespectful of the hearers. Much damage to the cause of Christianity was done, he argued, by the forms of presentation that contradicted the basic considerations of the faith.

For his own work, Kierkegaard did not use the direct method as his primary style. His reasons can be summarized as three. First, direct communication is not appropriate to the nature of the Christian religion. God has communicated with us indirectly, especially the supreme revelation in Jesus of Nazareth. God in human form is a paradox, an indirection, eliciting rather than overwhelming faith. If someone objected that Christ communicated directly on many occasions, Kierkegaard countered that because Christ was incognito, even his direct messages were indirect. The church is to use the paradox of the Incarnation as its model for word and action.

Second, because of the condition of Christendom, the direct method served only to add more information to that which already lay listless and useless on the minds of the hearers. "There is no lack of information; something else is lacking." Kierkegaard addressed a situation in which the content was known but not inwardly appropriated. To operate on the assumption that the listeners would be helped by offering them further increments of knowledge would, of course, only feed the illusion that the possession of information about Christianity makes one a Christian. There is a way of speaking and writing that demonstrates an imperialism of the mind and that engenders the same in the listeners and readers, as though an "I agree" or "I disagree" completed the transaction. With such an orientation one could even say "I agree I am a sinner" and remain aloof in the acknowledgment. Kierkegaard sought another method, one that would break the imperialism, with the listener or reader experiencing in every corner of mind and heart, "I am undone!" In the figure of the "professor," Kierkegaard personified the tendency to reduce life to ideas and to translate everything into objective knowledge. Kierkegaard's "professor" offers a course in which matters ethical are thoroughly treated, but in which nothing ethical ever occurs. There is information but not realization.

The third reason Kierkegaard rejected the direct method as his primary style is implied in the second: The direct method is not only nonproductive, but it is counterproductive. Kierkegaard understood that an illusion cannot be destroyed directly. Clerics who make direct attacks only create opposition, entrench defensiveness, and strengthen the illusion.[6] Religious orators who make direct accusations of sin pull up the wheat and leave the tares. "To thunder is no longer of any avail; it merely embitters men."[7] Kierkegaard even went further than simply pointing to the practical ineffectiveness of the direct approach. So profound was his respect for the inwardness of each person's life that he warned communicators: A truth spoken in subdued tones and embraced inwardly could become false when roared and shouted.[8]

Please notice that I have said Kierkegaard rejected the direct as his *primary* method. By that I mean not only that he preferred the indirect but that he did not totally dismiss the direct. Again and again Kierkegaard expressed genuine respect for science and the methods of objective research appropriate to investigations into areas of truth externally related to human existence. And the results of objective study can best be communicated directly. For example, a military instructor would best use the indirect method to draw out the soldier qualities in a recruit, but battlefield strategies and tactics would be taught directly. It is also sometimes the case that the indirect method needs to be preceded by the direct. Because indirection presupposes that the listener is in possession of that which is to be drawn out or evoked or stirred up, there are occasions when the listener must first be provided that raw material. It would be a mistake for an instructor or a preacher, fascinated by the indirect method, to employ it where the listeners were totally uninformed. The result could be little more than a psychological game. Even Socrates, master of the indirect method and, as we shall see, Kierkegaard's model, sometimes gave direct speeches to provide the substance for conversation and learning. Kierkegaard also anticipated that if the indirect method were successful in eliciting unrest, appetite, and capacity for personal appropriation of the truth that had long been known (but not inwardly), then communication could become direct, directly expressed and directly received.

A final reason, and the supreme one, for continued use of, and even necessity for, the direct method lies for Kierkegaard in the nature of Christian revelation. The truth with which we deal does not have its source within ourselves, as though the task of communication were to "bring out the best" or recover a native spirituality. Were such the case, the indirect style would be appropriate in every case from first to last. But Christianity centers in a historical revelation in Jesus of Nazareth. For this reason, a method appropriate to that fact—that is, the direct method—remains essential lest the Christian faith be consumed in uncritical and unexamined subjectivity.

One further word needs to be said before we give full attention to Kierkegaard's indirect method. It is not altogether the case that Kierkegaard's literary activity followed the pattern of beginning with the indirect and moving to the direct. This dynamic was at work, of course: first the indirect with its humor, irony, wit, and artistry, capturing the reader's attention in a kind of striptease to get them to come along; then the clear and simple word.[9] In this movement, the indirect served not only to create interest but also, as frequently was the case with Jesus' parables, to break up the encrusted soil of the religious community's assumptions, illusions, and calculations about the kingdom. But in addition to this sequential movement from indirect to direct, another dynamic was at work: The direct and indirect approaches to his readers occurred simultaneously. Delightful pieces, indirect in style and under various pseudonyms, appeared in print at the same time Kierkegaard published straightforward edifying discourses under his own name. He was not just playing games with his readers; Kierkegaard was serious, with reasons both personal and practical for such strategy.

Personally, Kierkegaard realized that he could not, nor could anyone else, negotiate life always by indirection. We need directness of relationships. Even Jesus, who by use of the parable indirectly related to and involved his auditors, at times spoke and acted directly, especially with those nearest him. "I am deeply grieved, even to death; remain here, and stay awake with me" is an appeal straight from the heart, without clever turns of the imagination. And Kierkegaard, fully realizing the contradiction involved, wrote *The Point of View for My Work as an Author,* explaining directly what he was trying to achieve in his indirect work. So strong was his need to remove the delicate screen of indirection that separated him from those with whom he shared what was dearer than life itself that Kierkegaard committed the violation against his work that he often predicted would be done by "professors": He *explained* it. Such was the final irony: It was as if the author appeared during each performance in his little theater and gave a running explanation of his work being performed.[10] The reason? In large measure, personal.

Practically, Kierkegaard offered his direct and indirect writings simultaneously because the contrast and tension provided by the direct was essential to the efficacy of the indirect. Kierkegaard was thus appropriating for Christian communication a principle commonly operative in classic stories and drama. For tragedy one does not paste dark on dark; rather, order and harmony must be clear background to revolt and chaos. For comedy, the significant and the serious are necessary raw material. Otherwise, you have not comedy but silliness. Or consider prophetic oracles in the Bible. The prophets, including Jesus, employed what we call debunking, designed to shatter the illusion of ultimacy that Israel tended to cast over the forms and institutions of her religious life. These oracles would have been mere shadowboxing were those forms and institutions not firmly and broadly entrenched. When protesting and debunking become the whole agenda, and therefore standard and predictable, they also become ridiculous.

So also with indirect methods used repeatedly and in the absence of the direct. Some years ago, the world of popular drama and literature experienced a revolt against the neat, well-ordered, happily-ever-after story, and in a fit of realism, writers treated us to the disordered, the formless, and the no-ending. It was a refreshing change; it caught on, then we were flooded with it. But without classes, recess is not recess.

Surprises become predictable; the unexpected is expected; and clever detours become familiar, well-worn routes to nowhere. Finally, everyone grows tired of it; the real loses its realism; and with the absence of tension caused by an overload in one direction, a new reversal begins.

In the New Testament, the most obvious indirect form is the parable. By means of brief narratives containing vivid and arresting metaphors, Jesus lured his followers into listening and then caught them in a new vision, a new perspective, an alternative way of seeing life and the kingdom. Within a widely and in places uncritically accepted tradition of direct correlation between sin and punishment, good deeds and rewards, obedience and divine favor, Jesus told of one-hour workers receiving full wages, derelicts at king's tables, parties for prodigals, and cautiously prudent servants being dismissed. Grace shatters the calculations of legalism and comes to us as a surprise. As a surprise, that is, until someone discovers those delightfully penetrating and incriminating stories and is so taken by them that all else Jesus said or did is neglected and these parables are shared endlessly. Not only are the tradition and context against which Jesus hurled these fragile bombs overlooked, but only those parables that contain a reversal or surprise receive attention. Stories in the gospel attributed to Jesus that are normal in cause-and-effect movement (foolish maidens are excluded; unfaithful servants are punished) do not qualify. Such is the downward turn that mars an otherwise elevating contribution by some recent researchers of the parables. And this unfortunate distortion is passed along to the congregations by those preachers who, fascinated by this biblical precedent for indirection and surprise, are now preaching surprises Sunday after Sunday to flocks no longer surprised. No church can thrive on a strict diet of O. Henry. Whether we learn it from Jesus or from Kierkegaard, the wise course to follow is to keep both direct and indirect—normalcy and reversal, justice and grace—present in the content and style of our communicating. The parables come to us in a context of other words and deeds of Jesus, who ministered in a world in which he was both citizen and alien. And the parables, puncturing and judging as they are, come to us within straightforward literary works called gospels. And so a parable within a gospel is a paradox, creating the tensions that contribute to the meaning of each.[11]

It is apparent that reasons for using direct and indirect methods in tension move beyond practical considerations to those of theological adequacy. The two methods are together more capable of carrying the paradoxical liveliness of the gospel. Which to employ more noticeably in a given situation depends heavily on the condition and expectation of the hearers. Keeping in mind that all listeners at times need no surprises, only support and consolation, let us pursue the polarities of direct and indirect a bit further. Under certain circumstances a direct approach could be as awakening and penetrating as an indirect in another context. Recall again the parabolic methods of Jesus as presented in the gospels. To certain listeners long conditioned by legal demands, a story of surprising grace might be given. To others beginning to include a rescue by grace in their calculations of the kingdom might come a story of straight justice. What a surprise!

I recall that in a class on the parables a few years ago, the students gravitated heavily toward the stories of a reversal type, in which the offer of grace was extended to the wayward son, the publican, the eleventh-hour worker, the servant who took big risks with the master's money. These students frowned on punishing lazy stewards or slamming doors in the faces of poor girls who forgot to bring oil. In short, grace was no longer unexpected, but expected by these seminarians and hence was no longer grace; or if it was, it was cheap. I read this story once without explanation and asked if it was a parable:

> There was a certain seminary professor who was very strict about due dates for papers. Due dates were announced at the beginning of a semester, and failure to meet them resulted in an F for the course. In one class three students did not meet the deadline. The first explained, "Professor, unexpected guests from out of state came the evening before the paper was due, and I was unable to finish it." "Then you receive an F," said the professor. The second student explained, "On the day before the paper was due, I became ill with influenza and was unable to complete it." "Then you receive an F," said the professor. The third

student, visibly shaken at the news about the fate of the other two, cautiously approached the professor's desk. Slowly he began. "Professor, our first baby was due the same day the paper was due. The evening before, my wife began having pains, and so I rushed her to the hospital. Shortly after midnight she gave birth to a boy. Our son weighs eight pounds. We named him Kenneth." The professor listened with interest, moved his chair back from the desk, and looked up at the ceiling. After a long pause, he looked across at the student and said, "Then you receive an F for the course." The news spread rapidly through the seminary. A large delegation of students came to the professor to protest. "Why have you been so cruel and harsh?" they asked. The professor replied, "At the beginning of the semester I gave my word concerning the papers. If the word of a teacher in a Christian seminary cannot be trusted, whose word can be trusted?" The students were dismissed.

Most of my students were angry not only with the professor in the story but with me for telling it. They insisted it was not a parable.

The point I am trying to make is that no one method or angle of vision can carry the word appropriate to every occasion. So Kierkegaard understood, and most likely the scriptures had convinced him of it, for in his work, as in the Bible, very dissimilar styles and messages are offered side by side. In Luke, for example, Jesus' offer of unconditional grace ("God is kind to the ungrateful and the wicked") is extended alongside a recurring call to repentance. The two messages are not interwoven, logically related, or homogenized. The reader has to wrestle with both words; neither can be discarded or discredited.

I am sure you have been struck, as I have, with the similarities in the contexts in which Jesus used parables and Kierkegaard used indirect discourse. Both Judaism and Christendom rested on traditions that provided the assumptive worlds of the audiences and the speakers. Those traditions were of such age and authority as to make the parabolic and indirect methods not only permissible but necessary. Just as Kierkegaard did not recommend the indirect method to missionaries on frontiers where there was no such tradition, so it is noticeable that Paul, for whatever other reasons, did not use parables to preach where no one had yet laid a foundation. The indirect method of communicating needs the direct for keeping the process alive, and it needs what the direct offers—information—in order to give substance to the process.

Now, let us look more carefully at Kierkegaard's method of indirect discourse. The teacher par excellence who was always the model for Kierkegaard was Socrates. Socrates had a communication problem not unlike that of Kierkegaard in that both men faced a situation in which the truth was known. For Socrates, it was known in each person's soul, because the soul is immortal and has from preexistence already a knowledge of truth. Learning is therefore recollection, bringing forth out of self the essential truth about self and life in the world. This recollection is not easy, because memory has grown fuzzy, buried under increments of false knowledge and illusions about self. It follows that one cannot, therefore, acquire knowledge from a teacher. Socrates saw his task to be one of helping to remove the hindrances of misunderstanding in order to awaken and evoke the truth within. The task was a delicate one because his listeners knew and yet did not know. Most communicators speak to those who know in order to be approved or to those who do not know in order to teach. But for Socrates, and for Kierkegaard after him, the effective method is maieutic; that is, after the manner of a midwife who helps to bring forth.[12]

What Socrates sought to achieve by questions and answers, Kierkegaard sought by what he called indirect discourse. Kierkegaard, like Socrates, worked on the assumption that the truth was known, and, therefore, no communication of knowledge was needed. What was lacking was the intimate realization of the significance of what was already known. Unlike Socrates' doctrine of the essential truth being present in each soul, Kierkegaard's essential truth was in the revelation of God in Jesus Christ. But this "information" had been so often and so repetitiously taught and preached that everyone in Denmark knew it. But in a deeper sense they did not know it. "In the community of Christianity, where the situation is qualified by Christendom, there is no direct or straightforward relationship, inasmuch as a vain conceit has first to be disposed of."[13] That vain conceit lies in the illusion that "knowing about" is knowing. To break that illusion, one does not add quantities of more information; rather, one stirs up and elicits what is there, taking away in order that what has been so often heard can truly be heard. The process could be compared to the sanding of a floor that has been painted many times and many colors. With the removal of paint, the beauty of the wood beneath again appears. Or to use Kierkegaard's own analogy, borrowed from Socrates, he became a midwife. He wrote to be an impetus, the occasion for inward appropriation of truth already at hand. One does not agree or disagree; one is affected or one is not.

In his briefest statement on the maieutic method, Kierkegaard probably puts it most clearly: "To stand alone with another's help."[14] "To stand alone": That was the goal, not dependent on Kierkegaard or clergy or institution, but before God to have the inwardness of faith. For all his readers Kierkegaard desired this, but they could not attain it simply by reaching inside themselves for the clarity of truth and the strength of trust. The illusions of Christendom were not so easily broken. "With another's help": That was Kierkegaard's task, delicate and difficult, for not only did the illusions have to be shattered, but this had to be done so as not to create disciples and satellites around himself. If that occurred, there would only be a shift of dependencies but no standing alone.

If Kierkegaard's method of communication is to serve more than our historical curiosity, we ought to pause here and make sure we are clear about what is implied and assumed about both listener and speaker (or reader and author) in the style being explored. For the listener, there is in the indirect method complete respect. The listener is respected for what is already known. Kierkegaard found his principle for proclamation in 1 John 2:21: "I write to you, not because you do not know the truth, but because you know it." The listener is respected for being in possession not only of the mental capacity for understanding what is being said but also of the appetites and capacities for living fully. Kierkegaard appealed to the full range of human faculties for joy, anxiety, love, purpose, meaning, and longing for eternity. Whoever brought to his writings a good set of healthy instincts was soon engrossed and captured. Kierkegaard understood about his readers what the more recent Christian writer C. S. Lewis understood:

> We are all prompted by the same motives, all deceived by the same fallacies, all animated by hope, obstructed by danger, entangled by desire, and seduced by pleasure...The main of life is, indeed, composed of small incidents and petty occurrences: of wishes for objects not remote and

grief for disappointments of no fatal consequence, of insect vexations...impertinences...of meteorous pleasures...Such is the general heap out of which every man is to cull his own conditions.[15]

This is respect. Kierkegaard did not insult his readers with prefaces warning them to be on guard or with conclusions that drew innocuous lessons and made oversimplified applications. This method also respects the privacy of the listener. Those who make direct charges and accusations in public gatherings, if heard at all, hurt and embarrass. But the indirect approach draws out the listener's own thoughts and feelings, which may accuse and convict, but if so, it is with a privacy that permits confession of wrong to God. As Kierkegaard put it, the indirect approach "shyly withdraws (for love is always shy) so as not to witness the admission which he makes to himself alone before God—that he has lived hitherto in an illusion."[16] And finally, the listener is permitted room to make the decision about his or her own existence. That decision is the act that is the end and goal of all Kierkegaard's art. Reasoning and reflecting can clarify issues, but resolution lies in the listener's venture and decision. Without that decision, discussions and clarifications, however brilliant, are as useless as sewing without knotting the thread.

And what is assumed about the speaker? Kierkegaard's observations are basically two. First, the speaker is in no way exempt from the struggles that characterize the life of the listener. Kierkegaard likened some preachers to swimming coaches standing on the dry dock shouting instructions to their charges, but not expecting anyone really to jump in. In fact, if one were to plunge in and start toward the deep, the coach would be frightened and threatened.[17] As a matter of fact, many parishioners do not want the minister involved in the life realities that they know. To them the preacher is a speaker, a performer, an actor. Suppose an actor continued after the curtain fell to be what he was in the play. He would be declared mad.[18] And what of the minister who continued on Monday in those matters about which she spoke eloquently on Sunday? The people would have no more of such a madperson. When people call for a leader who is "one of us," they are not telling the whole truth!

I want to pause here to tell you about Rachel, but I am very hesitant. She is so quiet, and her life has been so hidden from public view that such exposure as this brief story will bring might embarrass her. Rachel recently entered a retirement home, where others can be to her the family she never had. After graduation from normal school, she took a teaching job in the grade school of a small town, and there she remained for forty years, introducing children to books and ideas and to one another.

Before retirement she had taught boys and girls, and their boys and girls, and their boys and girls. Of course, she threatened to retire many weary springs, but threats by Rachel were very much like children's threats to run away from home. The fact is, she was pained by springtime and the simple rituals of promotion by which her boys and girls were lost to her. She felt delightfully guilty when a favorite pupil (Weren't they all?) was detained another year. Summers and weekends were spent gathering objects to help her teaching. I wonder how many pumpkins, flags, witches, turkeys, Santa Clauses, and valentines she had stuck on her classroom windows.

No one could have been more shocked than Rachel when the chairman of the school board told her that she was being given early retirement. Do not misunderstand— she never for a moment took it as personal criticism or a lack of confidence in her abilities as a teacher. Her response was shock simply because it vibrated against her final achievement of the one ambition of her life—to become a child. Not childish, that sad state of those who try to negotiate adult life with a child's reasoning and behavior. No, I mean she became a child. Rachel moved totally out of the adult world into that of the child. A child's laughter, fears, anticipations, games, pains, friendships were hers. At Halloween, at Christmas, on Valentine's Day, she was totally a child. Finally she had done it! No more generation gap, no more distance in vocabulary and perspective and vested interest; she now knew full rapport and perfect communication. "Poor Rachel," said the adults who had once been her pupils but who had so completely moved out of the child's world that they did not recognize in her present manner the full flowering of those childlike qualities she possessed only in part when they were in her class. But finally, after forty years, for the sake of the children, she had become one of them. The perfect teacher!

"She will have to be retired," muttered the school board to itself. "For the sake of the children we will have to let her go." No parent raised an outcry; they accepted in silence the decision as painfully right. Only a newcomer, with more reason than feeling, asked why. "Because she has become like the children." (And Jesus became in every way as we are; of course we had to get rid of him.)

Second, while the speaker is very much involved in the issues of his or her own existence, in no way is the speaker to become a model or seek attention whatsoever. The passion for enabling the hearer to appropriate the truth is such that the communicator is consumed, disappearing to help others become. Toward that end the speaker sacrifices whatever admiration and praise might otherwise have come, at times appearing naive, nonserious, lacking in dignity and that air of superiority that people have come to expect of the gifted and capable. Being anonymous or hidden behind pseudonyms did not detract, Kierkegaard reasoned, from the efficacy of his writings any more than biblical materials were less forceful or less authoritative because most of the authors are unknown.

Because Kierkegaard chose not only to use the indirect method but also to discuss it with his readers, we have from him a number of vivid analogies by which he described his literary efforts. It may be helpful to recall here images that were briefly mentioned earlier. In one image he saw his readers as persons having taken too much food (information) into their mouths. His task was to nourish them by taking away, not offering more. In a similar figure, he called his work the spice for the food, not the food itself, thus warning against a diet of Kierkegaard alone. Or again, he was to serve as a smoke consumer so that what was already there could be seen. In the same vein, Kierkegaard compared the religious situation of Denmark to a palimpsest, a parchment that had been written on repeatedly, text over text, so that the original message was obscured. His purpose was to apply the caustic acid that would bring to light the hidden text. He wrote, especially at the beginning, as a likeable scoundrel, generating interest and attracting many readers, some of whom would, he knew, be disaffected as he moved more directly to Christian subjects. Most of Kierkegaard's analogies had to do with the fact that the indirect approach slipped up on his readers, luring or deceiving into the truth. He referred to himself as a spy in a higher service, an infiltrator behind the enemy lines, one who attacked from behind and wounded to heal, one who seduced to save.[19]

But none of these analogies should be taken as implying that Kierkegaard was just playing with his readers. He knew the temptation that comes only to those of keen minds, rich imaginations, and superb skills of communication. "Without God I am too strong for myself," he confided, and therefore never let his own relation to God fall into disrepair.[20] If he were a spy, he was himself always under inspection; if he convicted others, he was himself always under arrest. As Socrates had humbled himself as an ignorant one in order to draw out the truth, so Kierkegaard wrote and spoke as one who was not a Christian in search of what it is to be Christian. In his writings he addressed himself; in relation to his own literary activity he was "a reader."

It is important to remember that indirect discourse was for Kierkegaard an overall strategy that permitted, even invited, within it a wide range of tactics. Contrary to many writers or speakers who have predictably familiar formats and styles, Kierkegaard communicated with many moods and modes. To have done otherwise would have dashed immediately any hope for a new hearing of the gospel. But first, of course, he had to possess what Abraham Heschel has described as prophetic insight, that breakthrough into the way things are. This required intellectual dismantling and dislocating, which comes only to those who engage a phenomenon with a feeling for the unfamiliar and the incredible.[21] And then, to communicate it. How? How can the immediacy of one person's experience become immediate to another? "The ideal requirement of Christian speech consists of this...It must not only talk *about* the listener's situation between the twin possibilities of offense and faith, but must place him in that situation—and in order to do this it must first create that situation."[22] We will talk of this in some detail in the next chapter.

Fully aware of the criticism that he was not a serious theologian, Kierkegaard kept his language alive—now playful, now serious, and most often both at the same time—as a farmer who has learned that by pressing and lifting on his plough at the same time he is able to make a deeper furrow. With a style reminiscent of the parables of Jesus, Kierkegaard wrote with homely familiarity, humor, exaggeration, distortion, vividness, and always in images. He understood that people live in images rather than ideas and that human transformation occurs when images carrying deep symbolic force are modified or replaced by others. By placing the strange in a familiar setting or the familiar in a strange setting, Kierkegaard walked the edge of language, to use van Buren's phrase, and evoked fresh experiences. As Paul Holmer has said of C. S. Lewis, he took the stuff of our world and arranged it so the reader would attend and intend the world differently.[23]

Two useful weapons in Kierkegaard's literary arsenal were humor and irony. These were not artifices imposed, because both are rooted in the contradictions of existence. Both the comic and ironic provide "oases of momentary disengagement" for objective observation and reflection.[24] Readers and listeners are thereby given room at an awkward and unsettled time when they may actually change their lives in the face of new insights. Writer and reader, speaker and listener, can both be incognito for that critical moment when privacy has to be maintained in order to make a decision. With a touch of humor a speaker can, in an emotionally charged moment, free a listener to ponder the issues raised. Without it the only alternative is resistance and defensiveness. By seeing the humor in earnestness and the earnestness in humor, Kierkegaard offered his readers point and counterpoint, permitting a decision, which is the only human way of demanding a decision.

We are, of course, talking about artistry. Art implicates and involves the reader, listener, or observer in ways more complex than agreeing or disagreeing. One's world, one's values, one's lifestyle can be confirmed or called into question by art when plain prose descriptions would pass as information, leaving life untouched. Of course, poetic and metaphorical language can serve as a disguise for embryonic and vague thinking, but on the other hand, a bit of artistry can lay hold of heart and mind and not let go until thoughts and feelings long dormant are stirred. "The king is dead; long live the king!" That not only makes sense, it makes more than sense. "He ain't heavy; he's my brother." Is that a legitimate way to talk in serious discourse? In "Thirteen Ways of Looking at a Blackbird," Wallace Stevens says, "It was evening all afternoon." That is not just a thought; that is an experience that evokes the reader's experience, and communication moves from image to image. Some call it art and reserve it for drawing rooms; Kierkegaard called it indirect discourse and with it made fresh again among those tired of it the subject of the Christian faith.

The language of faith has to move beyond the narrow range of concepts and ideas if life is to be tuned to God.

But not without troubled spirit, grave misgivings, and haunting fears. No amount of ability or genius exempts one from the inner struggles that never depart from those who communicate matters of ultimate concern. In fact, the larger the talent, the larger the conflicts; there are no sea storms in roadside puddles. In his *Journals,* first written for his own eye with no thought of publication, Kierkegaard made entries more than once about fears that hovered over all his literary activity. One fear he put as a question to himself: "Have I the right to use my art to win over a person?"[25] The question is one that hangs around every class in public speaking, every school of forensics, every course in homiletics, every program in evangelism. But it was an especially piercing question for Kierkegaard for two reasons. First, he knew his own unusual gifts as a communicator and therefore had to face the ethical issue of the use of this kind of power. Second, Kierkegaard was a private person, possessing a large interior world that was a sanctuary for him, and he had immense respect for the privacy of others. He tiptoed up to the door of another's heart and knocked softly. He cherished the distance that writing served to put between himself and others.

Speakers do not have this distance, and therefore have to create it, if they desire it, with their styles of communicating. This respect for another's privacy coupled with the theological position that every person is responsible for his or her own faith moved Kierkegaard toward the indirect method. Although he sometimes wondered if it were not the style of a coward, and yet for all the possible misuses of it available to every charlatan, he still regarded it as the most Christian method. The reader was never insulted; his knowledge of Christian teaching was respected; and the right of personal decision was never violated. Even so, like many others who have devoted tongue and pen to the service of the gospel, Kierkegaard always had the preference of remaining silent. He longed for a day on which he had nothing to say. The day never came because he knew, as you and I do, that communication is not something you may or may not do with the gospel; communication is a part of the very nature of the gospel.

A second fear that ate away at Kierkegaard was really a troublesome doubt, a question as to whether the pleasure he got from his work was a clue that he was swerving from the straight and narrow. There is no doubt that Kierkegaard found joy and at times unutterable satisfaction from the exercise of his rich imagination and literary skills. But he realized that such delight could become indulgence, and in that indulgence could occur lapses in purpose, losses of that message that made pregnant his thought and gave a reason to his literary activity. Were such a departure to occur, it would not be the common fault of reducing the quality of the product to appeal to general taste, but rather that of a literary conceit, a preoccupation with beautiful wrappings.

A third fear that surfaces throughout Kierkegaard's work is different from the other two mentioned above in that this one did not plague his own work, but had to do with what would happen to his writings after his death. In fact, this was not so much a fear as a dread, a painful awareness of what he knew would happen— his works would fall into the hands of "professors." The professor was for Kierkegaard the villain in Christendom, for the professor gathered information *about,* lectured *about,* knew *about,* and from his prestigious position had the influence to sustain the monstrous illusion that knowledge about Christianity is Christianity. And Kierkegaard, especially in his indirect discourses, labored endlessly to break that illusion, to make the transition from information about the faith to experience of the faith. He made himself the Socrates of Christendom, the occasion, the temporarily useful midwife, the self-liquidating teacher who effects that learning that consists of experiencing what one already knows. But Kierkegaard knew that after his death, the professor, with insatiable appetite for lecture material and with demonic genius for transforming all of life into sentences, would consume him. He had nightmares in which students at the university investigated what Kierkegaard "really meant," while professors arranged his thoughts under topics and joined with the clergy in making a good living teaching about Christian suffering.

The writings of Kierkegaard carry the faults as well as virtues of an effort to correct excesses in the church of his time. He called on those who followed to correct his corrections, for corrections addressed to one occasion parroted to a subsequent occasion are not just ineffectual, they are foolish oddities. No one wants her words to be grossly misquoted by being quoted exactly. Those of you who teach and preach know the feeling of cringing at the sound of some glib tongue quoting what you said. In fact, the experience of reading through one's own sermon or lecture of ten years ago can be embarrassing and not, as some suppose, because of ten years of improvement beyond that primitive and awkward effort. That lecture or sermon had an appropriateness that it no longer has. As a rule, the better the sermon or lecture, the shorter its life. Kierkegaard did not, nor do we, seek to communicate timeless truths; the desire is for the proper word, the word that fits here, now. If the next generation finds it strange or irrelevant or even laughable, so be it. But one still flinches at the thought.

6

To a Proposal: The Experience
of the Listener

*Something else is lacking, and this is a something which
the one cannot directly communicate to the other.*

I am afraid that the long route to a proposal has put on me the
burden of fulfilling a promise enlarged by the delay. Let me make
a few comments about what I am calling "a proposal." First, if
you discover that you have already anticipated much that is
offered here, I am pleased. It would be most satisfying to know
that these reflections served as a rubric under which to gather
your own good instincts about communicating. It is often the case
that courses in public speaking, teaching, and preaching inhibit
the flow of natural discourse and divert our energies into channels
that seem to be improvements over nature because they bear the
seal of esteemed professors and register credit on university
transcripts.

The best instruction in communicative skills, however, draws
out, encourages, and maximizes those arts we develop in the

various forms of ordinary social exchange. Some ministers I know still feel guilty, twenty years after seminary, when they preach with styles not blessed by a homiletics class. I know it is quite helpful at times not to be hit with a brand new approach but to be confirmed in the rightness of some avenues already taken. If to some of you what I suggest is a new idea, let me say that my urgings about it are designed not to persuade you to let my notions erase your board and replace your own habits but to convince you to let these suggestions take a place among the methods of communicating you employ. Most methods, however exciting and promising, are most effective when used selectively and among a variety of styles. Most methods under severe attack just now have the common fault of being the one style for every subject and occasion. Appropriateness and congeniality between form and content brighten the prospects of even the oldest and most commonly used methods. No one wins all races with the same horse.

All of you will be aware of the extent to which this proposal has been nourished and at points given some shape by the methods of discourse used by Kierkegaard. These next few pages will remind you of the last few. Good. But let memory serve as the link to the preceding discussion of Kierkegaard rather than entangling ourselves in cross-references. What Kierkegaard said and what I am saying serve properly not when the reader feels adequately informed, but when the reader is prompted, stirred, released, to more effective communication of the gospel that may or may not bear resemblance to these descriptions.

Of course, even if I so desired, Kierkegaard could not be uncritically transported and reduplicated on our occasions of teaching and preaching. The reasons do not all lie in the many kinds of distance between us and mid–nineteenth century Copenhagen. A major reason is that Kierkegaard's method of discourse was designed for writing, not for speaking. He was a guest preacher on a number of occasions, but his sermons did not carry the indirectness and the dialectic of his writing. His preaching was the sometimes poetic and always insightful unfolding of texts of scripture. But Kierkegaard was primarily a writer, and the relationship between writer and reader is quite different from that of speaker and hearer, even if a writer uses an oral style. Between writer and reader are a distance and a freedom that are not built into a speaker/hearer relationship. The writer is anonymous. The reader is in total privacy and in that privacy can move at any pace desired and can make a wide variety of responses without public view, pressure, or embarrassment. Neither have to be concerned about those traits of personality and appearance that may aid or hinder communication. The reader is free to regard the entire volume as written for someone else and therefore without any infringement on personal values or lifestyle, or the reader may feel inescapably addressed. A book may create and sustain a mood that gathers up the reader, or the reader may remain in a mood that resists the book. The burden of the writer is to give the book a kind of autonomy that by its form and movement and subject matter does its work: informing, persuading, entertaining, disturbing, or whatever. Except through words and phrases the writer has no access to the reader, and it is not known if those words and phrases are reaching the reader on an airplane, in bed, at a desk, or in a hospital waiting room.

Between a speaker and listener these conditions do not exist at all or, in cases, only partially. The speaker and listener are together in time, place, and common purpose, a fact that, while seeming an advantage to communication, may be a detriment. For example, being in the same room may blind the speaker to the wide range of thoughts, feelings, and private purposes that make speaker and listener not together at all. And thus, the speaker may proceed without first creating a situation or mood or "dwelling place" for the participants. Again, the speaker is often lured into thinking that personal presence, voice, force of personality, and oral delivery are such unambiguous advantages over writing that care in word choice and phrasing slips considerably. To be sure, these advantages can be great, but do not forget the many variables that can erode communication. Beyond that, keep in mind that as a reader before a book I am anonymous, free, not threatened, in private, and able to pace myself according to mood, intensity of involvement, intellectual demand, and circumstances. As a listener before a speaker these conditions do not prevail, unless the speaker has the insight, empathy, and skill to create them. Otherwise, I may be defensive, making sure I remain totally in charge of my own thoughts, feelings, and values, especially if it is evident that the speaker is capable. If the speaker is a dullard, two pleasures are mine: to sleep during the presentation and to complain afterward.

Do not anticipate that I am leading to the suggestion that we put all we have to say in print and let it be read. No one questions the lively values of personal interchange between speaker and listener as well as the benefits shared by a group commonly engaged, but has not Kierkegaard teased us into seeing the communicative values of distance, of privacy, of a kind of anonymity that gives us freedom to reflect and decide out of public view, of trusting form and content rather than personality and social pressure to achieve the desired ends? In other words, in addition to the advantages that belong to speaking/hearing experiences, is it not possible to capture also some that belong to writing/reading? I am persuaded it is. And if the conditions under which we do our teaching and preaching resemble Kierkegaard's Christendom enough for us to assume prior and repeated exposures to the Christian tradition, then the evocative powers of the indirect method in Kierkegaard's writings compel us to try. What is called for is ascertaining the dynamic at work and seeking to recreate it. The place to begin is with the reader/listener experience. That is the alpha and omega of the whole effort. Once we have grasped something of the listener's experience, we will then proceed to talk of ways the teacher/preacher can work to effect that experience.

If I may call the reader of Kierkegaard a listener, the word that best describes the listener's experience is *overhearing*. This is not Kierkegaard's word for it, but it is not difficult to demonstrate that overhearing characterized very important and sometimes decisive periods in his own life and therefore characterized what he hoped would occur for his readers. To begin with, Kierkegaard was a reader of many books, in the company of which he was comfortable, free, and without fear of invasion of privacy. Reading is, of course, an experience of overhearing. The messages in the books are addressed by the authors to someone else or to no one or to everyone. If in reading a book I cease overhearing and begin hearing a word addressed to me, it is because I appropriated the word rather than being coerced. The reader is always free to reflect, accept, reject, resolve. Even as a child, Kierkegaard discovered books to be more respectful of him than were other children, whose nicknames and taunts were often painful, and his own writing style later was marked by the freedom and respect accorded those who read him.

But overhearing the conversations of others was also a major part of Kierkegaard's daily routine. In the home, Kierkegaard's father had him sit with and overhear the discussions among the adults. Even in those periods when he withdrew from the social life of Copenhagen, he still kept up his sidewalk sauntering, not only engaging in conversation with passersby of every station in life, but also overhearing their talk with one another. These daily experiences were enjoyable for Kierkegaard, but they also provided insight, empathy, and vocabulary for his own literary activity.

One such experience of overhearing, casual and accidental, Kierkegaard was to recall years after it occurred as moving and unforgettable, decisive in its impact on his life. He was walking through a cemetery late one afternoon when from beyond a hedge he overheard an old man talking to his grandson beside the fresh grave of one who had been son to one and father to the other. Totally unaware of Kierkegaard's presence the grandfather spoke tenderly but forcefully of life, death, and life eternal. The substance of that conversation, not at all addressed to him, was formative for Kierkegaard's sense of mission, and the manner of his hearing it helped determine Kierkegaard's use of indirect communication. "It also became clear to me that if I desired to communicate anything on this point, it would first of all be necessary to give my exposition an indirect form."[1]

One can only guess the outcome if the substance of the old man's conversation with his grandson had been *directly* presented to Kierkegaard on the street, in a classroom, or in a sanctuary. Very likely there would have been only a discussion, perhaps an argument.

Kierkegaard sought to recreate for his readers the dynamics of his cemetery experience. Now he was the stranger, with no name or a pseudonym, expressing his inwardness to be heard by those who would overhear it. I say "overhear" it because he was not directly confronting the reader. At times Kierkegaard wrote as if addressing God, and the reader has the feeling of having stepped into a chapel thinking it vacant only to hear suddenly the prayer and praise of a solitary worshiper. In other writings Kierkegaard insisted that what was being said was addressed solely to himself. The readers overhear a man talking through very personal and very important matters with himself. And although he was primarily a writer, Kierkegaard was very much aware that the pulpit could also be the occasion for that impact that sometimes comes when hearing what has not been addressed to you. He noted in his *Journal* that the pastor who always sends remarks specifically and directly at the congregation is quite often not as effective as the pastor who speaks to them as though not speaking to them. A breeze moving over the listeners' heads sometimes quite forcefully stirs them.[2] At the close of *Either/Or*, Kierkegaard has a sermon. But rather than directly addressing the reader in the sermon, he offers it as a copy of a sermon by a young pastor in Jutland, a sermon that has not yet been preached. Thereby Kierkegaard sets up the occasion for our overhearing it.

I hope you are not resisting already the suggestion that there is potential for effective communication in the dynamic of overhearing simply because I have tied it closely to the experience and efforts of one, and he a somewhat unusual if not strange person. Were Kierkegaard the only ground for the case, then we would simply be talking over tea about a fascinating oddity with no general application. But Kierkegaard's value lies precisely in the fact that he had the uncanny ability to see into life and human relationships and observe the way things are. The reader of Kierkegaard says, "Of course; why did I not see it? Life, the world, people are really like that." Once the insight comes, it does not matter whether Kierkegaard or the apostle Paul or your plumber said it—it is true. So with our present consideration: Kierkegaard did not compose a truth about indirect discourse, and neither am I creating a new approach with a proposal about overhearing. I am simply asking that you observe how much effective communication takes place this way, in the experiences of others and in your own.

I have related the story of Kierkegaard's overhearing a conversation in a cemetery and how it affected him. Consider another, more generally familiar story. Under the date Wednesday, May 24, John Wesley entered a brief account in his *Journal*. He wrote of going unwillingly to the meeting of a society on Aldersgate Street, where one of the group was reading the Preface to Luther's *Commentary on the Epistle to the Romans*. Get the picture: went unwillingly; a stranger reading to a small group; and reading, of all things, the preface to a two-hundred-year-old commentary. Talk about overhearing! Not a direct, relevant, accusing, promising word addressed to Mr. Wesley. And yet, he says, "About a quarter before nine, I felt my heart strangely warmed." Or consider another. In book 8, chapter 12, of his *Confessions*, Augustine recalls the torment of his life when he was torn by the tug of the flesh toward the too vivid memory of his mistresses over against the quiet call of the Spirit of God. He was in Milan, sitting on a bench under a fig tree, his Bible open, but his vision dimmed by tears. He heard the voice of a boy or girl—he did not know which—calling out from a neighboring house: "Pick it up, read it; pick it up, read it." The voice was not, of course, addressed to Augustine; no doubt children were calling to one another in a game. Augustine, having stirred at the sound of a voice breaking his solitude, returned to the bench where he had left his Bible. He picked it up and read it. The passage before him was Romans 13:13–14, and as he read he was flooded by the light of full certainty as the gloom of doubt vanished.

Still too unusual and dramatic? Then let us move inside the sanctuary of your church and mine. Some of you can recall those extraordinary experiences of overhearing that came during evangelistic preaching services. The evangelist was usually a guest preacher, a stranger to us, and his sermons were addressed to the unconverted, the "prospects" in the room. Those of us who were members of the congregation overheard these sermons delivered in our presence by a stranger addressing other people. Many dynamics were at work, but one clear observation pertains: Sitting out of the line of fire, relaxed by the freedom and anonymity and distance, many church members found themselves stirred by what Kierkegaard called a breeze passing overhead. In fact, some testified to being more profoundly moved and renewed by the experience I am calling overhearing than when they were among the unconverted and the sermons were directed straight at them. Why? A number of good reasons have already come to your mind. I am tempted to pause here to make a suggestion to those preachers who are concerned to do preaching that is evangelistic. If sermons to the unconverted are heard effectively by those believers present who really overhear them, would it not be reasonable to assume that sermons addressed to the membership might be effectively overheard by any present who are not yet disciples? It is not only regrettable but sinful that visitors who overhear pastors speaking to the membership quite often find themselves listening in on announcements, scoldings, and faint pep rallies.

Or reflect for a moment on that phenomenon currently in vogue in many churches, the children's sermon. Early in the worship service the children are gathered at the front of the sanctuary where they are treated to a sermon designed especially for them. The pastor who does this effectively is oblivious to the adults present, a condition that works to the advantage of the adults. It is not uncommon to hear adults speak favorably of the children's sermon, some even preferring it to the main sermon of the morning. Of course, such talk is usually sprinkled with half-jests about being able to understand it or its being "on my level." There may be some truth there, but there is no doubt that a major factor beneficial to good communication is that the adults are listening to what is not addressed to them.

But the experience of overhearing does not pertain solely to certain styles of preaching; the worship service is filled with it. The prayers, of course, are overheard by the congregation. The pastoral prayer is not designed to be attended to closely by the worshipers, but to be evocative of their own prayers. Every one of us can recall hearing those sad pseudoprayers that were clearly addressed to the congregation, not to God. And Erik Routley has repeatedly reminded all of us that the offerings of choirs and instruments can be regarded as worship only if the congregation overhears them. Otherwise, it is a performance.[3] Is it too soon to ask if one could properly address a sermon to God, a sacrifice of one's lips, a doxology, with the worshipers permitted, as they so choose, to listen in? Maybe we should save the question until later, leaving our minds free just now to ponder other occasions in the communicating life of the church when overhearing is not a result of excluding certain persons from what has been called "target groups," but, on the contrary, is the dynamic that most properly respects the nature of the events and the privacy of the listeners. Recall, for instance, the funeral: Is it not a part of the minister's preparation to determine how and to what extent the bereaved family is to be addressed and in what ways they will simply overhear the word for the occasion? And those who attend a wedding know that except for a few opening "dearly beloved" comments, the entire event occurs between the minister and the couple. Everyone else has the sense of being present where something is happening that is big enough not to need any help. It is this sense that is so deeply moving, and you realize it by contrast when attending a wedding in which the minister treats the wedding party as props for his lengthy speech to the audience on "holy matrimony."

If we move outside the sanctuary, the experiences of overhearing that are occasions of very effective communication occur daily. I have spent evenings in alternating moods of applause and silence while a company of excellent musicians filled a hall with great sounds. I had the real sense that the grandness of the evening consisted in the fact that it was complete in itself—the music, the musicians, the hall—and nothing depended on me, on my presence, my agreement, my feelings about the whole thing. There was an announcement that it was going to happen, and I was privileged to be present. No one was in a lather to see that I was addressed or that everything was relevant.

Or an evening at the theater: What a powerful experience of overhearing that can be! For two hours I sit enthralled, disturbed, moved, called into question, amused, confirmed, angered by strangers who move about the stage talking to one another, seemingly unaware that I am there. No one walks to the edge of the stage and confronts me with life issues while maintaining good eye contact. No practical applications are offered, no final exhortations. Why is it, then, that I feel that I have been addressed and confronted and leave the theater with matters to think through again, matters that touch my life deeply? Through characters and lines alive with imagination and empathy, the play stirs the faculties with which I negotiate life, and by analogy and identification I become a participant. Sitting there alone in semidarkness, I am Kierkegaard in semidarkness in the cemetery.

Recall the play within the play *Hamlet*. Prince Hamlet knew that his uncle had murdered his father to take his place on the throne beside the queen. But he knew from the word of his father's ghost, and he could not bring charges of conspiracy and murder on the grounds that a ghost told him so. But when a troop of traveling players came to the castle, young Hamlet instructed them to perform a drama in which the central tragedy was a close analogy to the tragedy in his own family. Then Hamlet sat where he could observe his uncle during the play. Although no one directly accused him, the murderous usurper was trapped, caught in the lines and scenes of the play. He entered the palace theater to overhear, and he heard. It is, in my opinion, regrettable that some playwrights have not been willing to trust the dynamic of overhearing to enlist the audience and have resorted to more direct involvement of those present. For example, Arthur Miller's *After the Fall* is clearly directed to the audience, who must play the role of "the Great Listener" in this psychoanalytic confession.[4]

The experience I am describing is not unlike that of looking at great art. To be sure, the artist probably knew all along others would view the work just as the playwright knew audiences would see and hear, but part of the greatness of the art lies in its not having been painted for consumers. When the artist does not paint for me, the impact on me is greater. I will not take time to discuss how advertisers have sensed the value of this indirection and have been taking us daily into kitchens, laundries, and supermarkets, where we are allowed to observe unnoticed and to overhear the testimonials about mouthwash and vegetable oil. Constant repetition has a way of finally violating and insulting those who were at the outset almost persuaded.

It is my experience that a major factor in meaningful engagements with the Bible is overhearing. I have written briefly in this vein elsewhere and therefore will only touch on it here.[5] But think about it. Have you not gone to the scriptures demanding that they speak directly to you, yielding information or comfort or a lecture or a sermon for a fast-approaching occasion and, in reflection later, had to admit to assault and rape of the text? And yet, on other occasions, the distance provided by the anonymity of the writer, the alien time and place of the narrative, and the general feeling of "this is for someone else" dropped defenses, removed the threat that closes eye and ear, set you free, and hence permitted the Word to come to you. Much of the Bible is obviously to be overheard before it can be heard. Paul wrote letters, but not to me. Common courtesy dictates, therefore, that whether reading for personal edification or doing careful exegesis, I should stand back and let Paul and the Corinthians discuss the matter. I not only will learn a great deal this way, but I can trust that the text soon will reach out and, as happens when attending a good play, draw me onto the stage. Walter Slatoff has reminded us that the listener is both spectator and participant. Both distance and involvement are present.[6] In fact, distance tends to increase involvement, because without distance, involvement is too aware of self and may suddenly retreat and hide in self-consciousness, embarrassment, pain, or fear.

By contrast, consider the common experience of those who read Charles Dickens. At first, the reader learns, from a distance, a great deal about poverty and injustice in nineteenth-century England. Soon the reader moves closer to the story, begins to feel dismay and anger, and later, quite apart from Dickens, bears a new conscience and sensitivity about social ills.[7] What began as overhearing ended as hearing. The parables of Jesus were told to be overheard. "There was a certain man": anonymous, past tense, somewhere else, nothing here addressed to me. Relax and enjoy the story. And then it happens: I am inside the story, and the door closes behind me. Some of these parables are followed by interpretation, and the difference between reading the parable and its interpretation is noticeable. The interpreter has converted indirect discourse into direct, and moved the reader from overhearing to hearing. One does not have to be a literary critic to discern the shift from parable to interpretation.

It is not in the parable interpretations alone that indirect communication becomes direct. In New Testament materials that reflect intense polemic at work, the more casual indirect communication has been put in armor and placed on the front line of direct debate. Consider the difference between the reader's experience in the synoptics and in the gospel of John. Admittedly, with differing degrees of indirection and permitting the readers differing amounts of freedom and distance, the synoptic writers tell the story of Jesus. Conviction is expressed, to be sure, and the authors are proclaiming, but even so the reader has room for more than one response. There is no sense of being coerced; the call to discipleship is an invitation. Even though the evangelists shout from the housetops, something of the original whisper remains. There is still room for the offense of the gospel. Jesus is being talked about, and we overhear the conversations with him and about him. In the Fourth Gospel the dynamic of the experience changes radically; the reader is aware of direct confrontation. Conversations between Jesus and Nathaniel, Jesus and Nicodemus, and Jesus and the woman of Samaria, serve undisguisedly (as shifts in tenses and pronouns reveal) as occasions to launch sermons straight to the reader. What others were saying or implying about Jesus in the synoptics, Jesus says directly about himself in the gospel of John. "I am the way"; "I am the good shepherd"; "I lay down my life in order to take it up again." There is a world of difference in the listener's experience. Imagine two situations. In one, you hear testimonies about someone, and you then make up your mind about that person. In the other, that person tells you directly who and what he or she is: "I am—" Feel the difference? We are not getting into a christological dispute; I am simply wanting us to be aware of the kind of listener's experience that is generated by the method of communication we use.

There are signs that the reader's experience is beginning to receive attention as a dimension of New Testament scholarly activity. For generations some biblical scholars have demanded that the reader of the text come to it without any personal or historical baggage in order to hear without distorting the text. It makes good sense and delivers us from all manner of private psychologizing of the text. But might it not also be true that the reader's own prejudices, personal hungers and fears, and historical context could open up the past and aid communication with the writer and original reader, whose experiences and contexts were not all that different?[8] There can be as much distortion by distance as by participation in the text. And why do so many regard the intellect alone as keeper and carrier of the pure truth while emotions are always the villain? On the title page of volume 1, *Either/Or*, Kierkegaard copied two lines from "The Fourth Night" by Edward Young:

"Are passions the pagans of the soul?
Reason alone baptized?"

Simply stated, we need to remember that the Bible is literature, and granting what can be learned about it by source analysis, the impact a biblical writing makes is still a result of its present form. William Beardslee, for example, has reopened the field of literary criticism, not as a way to historical recovery, but as a way of looking at the main literary structures of the New Testament to see how they function religiously. Professor Beardslee realizes that distance from the texts is vital for clear and fresh perspective, but that imaginative participation in the scriptures is also necessary. He sees two paths to this participation or involvement: identification with the characters and events in the text, and dialogue with the texts. Out of fear that identification is too close to mysticism and could lead to loss of the historically objective quality, he prefers dialogue as the better method.[9] While this issue will arise again later, my present proposal is that there is a method of appropriating and communicating scripture that preserves the distance from the text necessary to its own integrity as a historical document and the participation in the text necessary to its faith and life function as the scripture of the church today. That method is overhearing. Overhearing scripture, as with music or drama or a good book, owes most of its power to these two factors: distance (I am an anonymous listener, reader, viewer, unrelated to the event) and participation (I am drawn in by identification with persons and conditions within the event). With the safeguard of distance there need be no fear of Professor Beardslee's mystic identification. More later.

If any of us are having trouble embracing the posture of overhearing as valid and vital for listeners to the Christian message, it certainly is not because we cannot recall experiences that verify it as effective communication. In fact, the texture and flavor of such experiences have more than once been occasions of refreshing relief from the overbearing and imperialistic styles of some teachers and preachers. I can certainly identify with Erik Routley's account of being reduced to mental paralysis by a tour guide who overwhelmed everyone with detailed descriptions of each historical site.[10] Tour guides have no monopoly on the fault; many speakers and writers are so exhaustingly complete that there is nothing left for the listener and reader to do. They do not seem to realize that there are occasions when it is better simply to touch the arm and say, "Over there is Arlington Cemetery," and leave it alone. Anyone who has barely survived a verbal massacre knows the truth in Kierkegaard's simple analogy: "In sawing wood it is important not to press down too hard on the saw; the lighter the pressure exerted by the sawyer, the better the saw operates. If a man were to press down with all his strength, he would no longer be able to saw at all."[11]

No, if we are having trouble with overhearing as a viable option among the possible listener experiences, it is very likely because of our being conditioned for decades to regard confrontation and direct address as the only communicative styles with honesty, integrity, and effectiveness. This style has taken over the domestic scene. Children who once were allowed to learn and have their imaginations kindled by overhearing parents and other adults have had that benefit removed. Either the children are not in the room, or they are being addressed directly. If children are present, the world of things and ideas is scaled down to fit; no breezes stir over their heads. They go to worship and hear a sermon addressed to children and then leave the sanctuary. No chance is given to lean against adult shoulders and hear words, observe motions, and sense emotions that create awe and wonder about something, someone bigger than children, bigger even than adults. Does everything have to be immediately understood and meaningful? An occasion for pondering these things in the heart is not, I think, a waste. When I was about six years old, I overheard elders pray beside the bed of my gravely ill father. There was so much I did not, and do not, understand, but I knew I was in the presence of something really big, much bigger than all my toys.

Of course, I am not pleading for the good old days when children were seen but not heard. That would be nonsense. But there is also some nonsense in our being so captured by the gains in a new method that the benefits of an old one are totally surrendered.

The encounter and confrontation models have come to dominate formal settings for communication. Chairs in a circle and eye to eye; that is where it happens and how it happens. We are all on the spot, addressing and being addressed. I hear you saying, and you hear me saying, and woe be to the person who tries to sneak in a little overhearing and maybe a bit of irrelevance. If the occasion calls for a formal presentation such as a lecture or a sermon, the key is "eye contact." Why? No one can argue that there are not kinds of material and types of messages shaped for eye contact, and to say these things with a wandering eye or distant gaze is to counter the message with the impression of unimportance. But it is just as true that there are kinds of material in a lecture or sermon that are violated by eye contact.

Many of my students come to seminary having been drilled by speech teachers to keep eye contact at all times, and these young preachers stare meaninglessly the same through argument, humor, anecdote, and casual story. A good storyteller seldom looks at anyone. Some whittle, some look into the glowing fireplace, some never stop walking down the lane, and others lie on the hillside looking at the stars while chewing tender stems of wild grass. They save their eye contact for those occasional didactic turns when there is a lesson to be planted on the forehead. But stories are always overheard, and in that overhearing there may well be encounter and confrontation. These are experiences of the listener, not tactics of a speaker who does not realize that some moments are allowed to happen, not made to happen.

In theological and biblical circles, encounter achieved the status of a canon by which to evaluate the scholarly enterprise. The "I-Thou" of Martin Buber breathed life into dogmatics and gave systematic theology, corralled in its own sentences and propositions, new freedom and a reason for being. The point of it all? The "I-Thou" encounter; no one would deny that. In biblical scholarship the dominance of historical research was broken by Karl Barth in the service of the sermon. This concern ran through all the work of Rudolph Bultmann and his students, who developed methods of biblical interpretation designed to set free the word of God as address, to effect for the listener the unmediated existential encounter. I do not have to laud here the many boons to the Christian community that began again, under this impetus, to hear sermons rather than history lessons, to recover some sense of the immediacy of the Spirit and contemporaneity with Christ, and not at the price of surrendering sound scholarship. Real gains accrued to the lay membership because of, not in spite of, genuine critical research. But even so, I do lament one serious loss. By defining the word of God as address, the experience of the hearer was contracted to a decision, an act of the will. The posture of confrontation gave no room for the happy accident of overhearing. "Once upon a time" capitulated to "once and for all."

And so it came to pass that the third person pronoun—*he, she, it*—slipped from the vocabulary of those teaching and preaching the gospel. The two legitimate pronouns were *I* and *Thou*, with *we* available for efforts at community. Of what value is the third person? it was asked. It is the pronoun of gossip (he said this; she said that) and of description (he did this; she did that). And is not description all we have been getting from historical critical scholarship (Israel did this; Paul said that)? The reaction was not to be denied; the time had come for confessional language (I) addressed directly to the hearer (Thou).

The result was a dichotomy: descriptive or confessional language, historical or contemporary. I do not have to tell you what errors follow such dichotomies. Some abandoned history for immediacy while others remained descriptive, refusing to let the present possess the past. In the meantime, theories of hermeneutics—how to negotiate the distance between past and present—multiplied, all of them promising to make winners of both sides. But can both history and contemporaneity be respected and satisfied in the teaching and preaching of the church? I think so. The two factors in the listener's experience—distance (history) and participation (contemporaneity)—are the two basic ingredients in the experience of overhearing.

It is possible, as any attendee at a play or reader of a book or listener to a story knows, for a speaker to be engaged in narration that is historical, descriptive, and third person, and for a hearer to identify, participate, and, if I may say so, be encountered. If the story is the right story, and if the teller narrates with insight and empathetic imagination, conscious of but not occupied with the listener, the one who overhears will hear. The *I-Thou* is in the experience of the hearer, not in the vocabulary of the speaker. The impact of the biblical narrative in the Christian community is a testimony to the fact that a "once upon a time" can be heard as a "once and for all." To abandon that narrative out of sincere desire to effect a "once and for all" experience is to have surrendered the arsenal and gone into battle with good eye contact.

Perhaps I caricature a bit. But I remember a few years ago sitting beside a man from West Germany and overhearing a Jew from England tell the story of a Jewish community in Poland. When the story ended, the German and I turned to each other, paused in silence, and moved out separately. Both of us had been addressed, confronted, encountered, called into question, and immensely assured in our hope. Distance? Yes; long ago and far away, about Jews, in Poland. Participation? Yes, we were there.

I am not asking for recess from vigorous direct communication so that we can all slump into a round of casual conversation. I simply wish to keep overhearing on the schedule of very important things to do. It is not, as we have seen, without power. And in a time of confusion over hermeneutics and how respect for both past and present can be preserved, it is not without merit.

But we have been talking about overhearing as an experience of the listener. The question that now arises is whether overhearing, for all its pleasant power, must remain one of life's happy accidents, its benefits all to be regarded as serendipity, benefits that vanish when we seek to contrive, construct, even urge. In other words, from the speaker's perspective, does any effort to effect overhearing become simply a maneuver, a maneuver that by its poor disguise is clearly artificial and hence counterproductive?

It is time now to address this question.

7

To a Proposal: The Method of the Teller

...which the one cannot directly communicate to the other.

The modest proposal being offered here is that the listener's experience of overhearing is a natural, effective, and at times life-changing dynamic that belongs in the church's classroom and sanctuary. And because it is also appropriate to the study, the transition from desk to pulpit or lectern is made less awkward and difficult. The discussion began with the perspective of the listener, not with the speaker's preparation or with the format of the content to be communicated. The reason was simple: With the listener is the place to begin. This has not always been the case. As we have observed, in the community of critical scholarship, the fear of the loss of objectivity and historical honesty made it seem essential that research and the reporting of that research be done with no consciousness of the existence of listener or reader. Otherwise, the listener's own needs and circumstances would add a variable to the investigations and color the results.

The point is, in a laboratory or in a library the gathering of listeners would be an intrusion, an interruption of the proper business conducted in those settings. But in a classroom or sanctuary, listeners are not intruders; they are as ingredient to the proper business of these settings as equipment and formulae in the laboratory or books in the library. And the proper business in classroom and sanctuary is communication. To that end the teacher or preacher is servant and instrument; to that end the subject matter is shaped and aimed.

It is vital to our task that we be aware that the experience of listening is not a secondary consideration after we have done our exegesis of the texts and theological exploration. The listener is present from the beginning. The Christian tradition, biblical and extra-biblical, came to us from those who *heard* it, and we *hear* it and pass it on to other *hearers*. The stamp of listening and the listenability of the message is on it when we get it, and in telling it, we confirm that it is listenable. To give such attention to the listener is not a concession to "what they want to hear," playing to the balcony or to the groundlings, nor is it an introduction to how to succeed as a speaker; it is no more or less than to describe the shape of the subject matter (it came from listeners) and the nature of the occasion (to effect a hearing).

Having begun with the experience of listening as the governing consideration in a communicative event and as the preoccupation that harnesses the imaginative, emotive, and cognitive powers of the speaker, I characterized that posture of listening called overhearing as consisting of two elements: distance and participation. Because the term and idea of distance may need rehabilitation, I have urged that we think of distance as that quality in a communicative event that preserves invaluable benefits for the message and for the listener. For the message, distance preserves its objectivity as history, its continuity as tradition, and its integrity as a word that has existence prior to and apart from me as a listener. In other words, the distance between the message and the listener conveys the sense of the substantive nature and independence of the message, qualities that add to rather than detract from the persuasive and attention-drawing power of the message. I am much more inclined toward a message that has its own intrinsic life and force and that was prepared with no apparent awareness of me than toward a message that obviously did not come into being until I as a listener appeared, and then was hastily improvised with desire for relevance offered as reason for the sloppy form and shallow content. These didactic and hortatory pieces are usually offered by well-meaning speakers who so highly prize relevance that they prepare their messages during the delivery. I do not wish to be sarcastic. My students who resist the lectionary and advanced planning for preaching with the retort "Who can know in January what will be relevant in June?" have a point, a good point, but a point that has its value only when held in tension with the gospel that is always beyond us: The word does not have its source in the listener. This is what I am calling distance, a necessary dimension of the experience of overhearing that says to the listener, "You are sitting in on something that is of such significance that it could have gone on without you."

As for the benefit distance provides the listener, we have talked of the room the listener has, room in which to reflect, accept, reject, and decide. As a listener, I must have that freedom, all the more so if the matter before me is of ultimate importance. As a listener who is also a teacher and preacher, I am aware that being armed with Holy Writ and the word of God tempts the communicator to think that the urgency and weight of the message call for pressing in and pressing down, leaving the hearer no room for lateral movement. But listeners worth their salt will soon, against this assault, launch a silent but effective counterattack: find flaws in the speaker's grammar or voice or logic or dress; raise questions about the speaker's real motives; wonder imaginatively if the speaker has a dark past or even at this moment is entangled in affairs illicit; make distracting body movements; count things, such as light bulbs, knots in wood, number of persons present wearing glasses, and so forth. I need go no further; your list of things to do when confronted with such a speaker probably is longer than mine.

The other element in the experience of overhearing is participation: free participation on the part of the hearer in the issues, the crises, the decisions, the judgment, and the promise of the message. Participation means the listener overcomes the distance, not because the speaker "applied" everything, but because the listener identified with experiences and thoughts related in the message that were analogous to her own. The fundamental presupposition operative here is the general similarity of human experiences. It is this that makes communication possible, but it is surprising that so many speakers do not trust this to be the case and feel it incumbent on themselves to supply descriptions of experiences as though they were foreign to the hearer. If both speaker and listener have observed an old man asleep in church, lengthy description is unnecessary; if not, lengthy description evokes nothing.[1] The story the speaker is telling and the personal story of the hearer must intersect at points, or the hearer will despair; however, if they are exactly the same, the hearer will be bored or suspicious or defensive.[2] Of course, the speaker who wants the listeners to overhear will preserve distance in narration, but the vocabulary, idiom, imagery, and descriptive detail will be such as will allow points or moments in the process at which the listener can "enter," identify, be enrolled. Otherwise, the listener cannot overcome the distance, and the communication, if attended to, becomes nothing more than shared information or a speech on a certain topic.

We probably need to pause here and remind ourselves again of those concrete examples of communication designed for overhearing, the narrative parables of Jesus. Recall or reread the prodigal son, the good Samaritan, the Pharisee and the publican, the workers in the vineyard, the talents, or any of the stories told with enough detail to have a narrative line. These parables are told in third person, in past tense, with anonymous characters acting and speaking in life situations distinct from the listener's. This is distance. But anyone who reads or hears these stories knows their power to enlist participation, both in the pleasure of the stories and in the inescapable demand they make. As Sallie McFague has pointed out, the parables take the mind *off* the very thing they put the mind on.[3] The hearer is free, and yet the response *permitted* is a response *demanded*. In hearing these stories, the listener overcomes the distance, perhaps surprised at the time, not because these are Bible stories but because the listener says, "Life is that way; I am that way; I have done that, felt that, thought that."

Now think of examples of communication that eagerly and sincerely seek the hearer's involvement and participation, but do so directly, without the counterbalancing element of distance. Who of us has not been exhausted and at times repelled by direct emotional and intellectual intrusions on our faculties, with all positive effects that might have been there consumed by the communicative effort itself? No matter how much a speaker pledges sincerity, shows feeling, and swears to genuine concern, a direct disgorging of emotion does not reproduce that same experience in me. Kierkegaard has already taught us: "Inwardness cannot be directly communicated...The direct expression of inwardness is no proof of its possession, but the tension of the contrasting form is the measure of the intensity of inwardness."[4] By "contrasting form" Kierkegaard meant that each quality of thought or emotion should be offered in tension with its opposite. For example, set earnestness in a context of humor, or humor in a context of earnestness. It is this same kind of tension between distance and participation that characterizes overhearing and contributes its dynamic. As restraint of emotion in a speaker makes it stronger in the listener, so distance enhances participation.

Back to the person at the lectern or in the pulpit whose task it is to bring about this experience of overhearing: Can something be done toward such an occurrence, or should we admit its elusiveness and be content to be surprised and pleased after the fact? Granting the elusiveness of any formula for effecting predictably another person's experience, and leaving large room for the activity of God's Spirit as well as countless other variables not of our doing or within our control, a few suggestions are in order.

Once it has been decided that a particular lecture or sermon, in toto or in part, will be most appropriately received by overhearing, begin early in the process to envision the style of delivery that will effect that experience. Having material to be overheard does not guarantee that such will be the case. I have been present when pastoral prayers, obviously meant to be overheard, were offered with the volume and tone of exhortation. Sermon materials commonly called illustrations are, among other purposes, to interest and to relax, and are to be overheard, but some preachers hardly get past "once upon a time" before they are sawing the air and "addressing" the listeners. To deliver a message for overhearing, the speaker needs to trust fully in the message to create its own effect, trust the listener to exercise freedom responsibly, and trust the process, however fragile and accidental it may appear, to be powerful. Voice, hands, posture, and face will testify to the presence of this trust.

Delivery goes a long way in creating what I have called distance, speaking *with* those present by not speaking *to* those present. This particular occasion is definitely not the one for using all that good eye contact you worked so hard to develop. There is a time and a message for that, but today is not it. In this presentation you may be talking to yourself or to God or to an imaginary group or to no one in particular—just remembering and reflecting. The eyes move about in the same general direction as the tongue; they do not confront or challenge or expose. The main thing is to create the mood, in yourself and in the room, for overhearing. It is not easy to do, because pressing, urging, exhorting, and challenging paw the ground, anxious to charge. The balance of energy remaining after the preparation is ready and anxious to be used in the proclamation. (I have observed that the less energy used in preparation of a message, the more there seems to be expended in its delivery.) We fear a casual atmosphere may give the impression of unimportant business.

Certain exercises may be helpful. For example, following those occasions in which overhearing was structured into the events, such as weddings and funerals, sit alone and re-experience the dynamic of it. Or in informal conversational settings, tell experiences and stories that have a "once upon a time" quality: "When I was in the third grade," "Years ago a blind man passed our door every morning," "There is a primitive tribe in the South Pacific that never sits down," "There was a certain man who had two sons." Stick with third person and first person, no second person. And of course, as nothing improves one's ability in speaking as listening does, frequent experiences of overhearing are invaluable. In addition to those that just happen, informal opportunities are provided by park bench storytellers, and formal opportunities are offered by the theater. Benefit from these occasions is multiplied by reflection on them afterward. One can also gain from reading the published prayers and correspondence of persons who obviously were writing to someone else. Here I do not refer to books that try to take advantage of the overhearing dynamic by assuming the form "Letters to Henry." The difference between such books written for the market and private letters composed with no thought of the public eye is enormous.

Similarly, addresses and sermons for particular occasions and audiences, however remote from your own circumstance, can be pleasant and often very moving experiences. Sermons preached to West Point cadets or to San Quentin inmates or to retirees at Sun City are ruined if for publication they suffer editorial tinkering to make them "relevant" for all the readers. I want to overhear them; in so doing I will hear what I need to hear. And I mention again overhearing Paul by reading his letters to friends and churches in other places at other times. Accept the distance between them and you, and enjoy reading this ancient correspondence. There is no need and no value in rushing in to intrude with your support for Paul or to join in yelling at the Corinthians. Stand back; you will be drawn in soon enough, and inescapably. Listen in at the door when Jesus is privately instructing the Twelve, or pause along the way and overhear his promises to the poor and disfranchised and his rebuke of blind, insensitive leaders. Stand back; Jesus does not need your Amen or your commentary. My experience has been that he gets around to me too soon anyway, even before I am finished with my own plans for myself.

I am convinced that a style of delivery for overhearing comes to the communicator who experiences, reflects on, is persuaded of the appropriateness and power of, and employs discriminately, this dynamic. Voice and frame will announce loudly if it was a clever Saturday night notion. Effectiveness increases as comfort with it increases, as it comes to fit the contours of your self, much in the manner of an old sweater. I have nothing to say to a person who is looking for something cute, something that will really "get them." Kierkegaard believed that "everyone who really has thoughts has also style immediately."[5] I do not doubt it, for with a certain idea comes also an early feeling for the form in which that idea would be most at ease. Some lectures and some sermons say quite clearly to the communicators, "This they cannot hear except by overhearing."

A second suggestion to the communicator who may embrace this proposal has to do with sacrifice, the willingness to structure one's message so that it is consumed in the experience of hearing it. If I genuinely give myself, my faculties of mind and heart, to effect something, to generate, or to activate something within the lives of the listeners, then my message and not just my life in some general sense will function as such a servant. This is not a perspective to be quickly or easily embraced. Jesus was not a servant solely in the sense of healing or foot washing; his manner of teaching was servantlike in that he *gave his speaking* to effect experiences within the listeners. Here is the Son of God using anecdotes, stories, paradoxes, contradictions, humor, irony, question and answer. Is that the stuff of revelation from on high?

It is not the performance that gains tenure or renews contracts. Jesus laid himself open to criticism from even the sophomore class in a rabbinic school, criticism as to scholarship, logic, and systematic consistency. Why did he do it? He gave himself in this sense also, that his communications were servants to awaken, to arouse, to provoke, to assure. Bring to them other canons by which speeches or lectures or sermons are ordinarily measured, and his are hardly classic orations.

But Jesus was not a speaker or orator; he was a teacher whose style was forged to bring about an experience in the listener. Socrates was a teacher, and he gave himself to teaching. He served his students by meeting them where they were. To nonstudents he seemed ignorant, lacking in dignity, spending too much time on mundane, everyday matters. To his students, once the Socratic method functioned to stir truth and insight within them, he was dispensable. Kierkegaard had a mission, to awaken Christianity within Christendom, and to do that he employed wit, humor, irony, homely stories, pseudonyms, a strange lifestyle, philosophical discourse—whatever tools a genius could assemble. Of course, he was open to criticism as to the health of his mind, his psyche, and his body.

I never cease being awed by anyone who can be so completely giving of self to the listeners. Most of us are too aware of those in our balconies observing our performances whom we wish to please or impress: family, former teachers, peers. How large an obstacle is the ego, and especially in the path of communication! Why is it that we find it easier to let financial resources, time, or physical energy be servant to the gospel than we do our speaking? Is it because we reserve our manner of speech to protect ourselves and our image and to create the proper impression or to correct a wrong impression? After all, our speaking and writing are practically the only means we have to demonstrate that we have an education and some understanding. Since such qualities do not show in appearance or income or friends, then our words are called on to keep sentinel watch over our image and, on occasion, prove something to someone. As long as our speaking and writing serve these ends, they refuse to *give themselves* to listeners, sacrificed in the service of a mission to those who have heard repeatedly but do not really hear. It has more than once occurred to me that all the attention on the minister as servant seldom focuses on his messages as servants, spent, used up, consumed in service to the listener.

You know as well as I that I am not calling for anti-intellectual, undisciplined, casual playing to the public and "just giving them what they want." The point is, overhearing is an experience of the listener, and if I give myself to the effort to bring that to pass, I have to *give myself* to bring it to pass. I am the narrator, the enabler, and if I start thinking of the impression I am making or my position or my consistency or my scholarship, the listener's experience is aborted and the audience begins to agree or disagree, approve or disapprove, praise or criticize the speaker—all rather useless responses.

There is a way of presenting a message that can be "consumed by the listener," a desirable goal if one is convinced that the meaning for a listener is not a product at the end of the event but rather, that meaning is coextensive with the process of listening. We may be helped in understanding by the distinction between rhetoric and dialectic in Plato.

Rhetoric satisfies the listener, and at the end of a rhetorical presentation, the listener says, "That was a good speech." As a speech it is an identifiable entity; it has form and substance and can be repeated as is or printed and published. Dialectic, however, disturbs a listener toward a kind of conversion of thought or values or life direction, but it proceeds at its own expense. As it effects an experience in the listener, the presentation itself is used up. The early part of it moves you on to the next part, which may cause you to lose interest in or abandon the earlier part. And so the entire presentation proceeds. If effectively done, the listener could hear the earlier portions of the message repeated and be uninterested or even reject them. Why? Because the words and sentences and images moved the listener along in changing views or values; as those words did their work, they died. They were not framed to carry a truth statement or a position on a doctrine, but they were in the service of the listeners, to the end that what remained after the occasion would not be "a good speech," but a listener modified or changed or at least beginning to experience anew old notions fast asleep in the soul.[6]

Stanley Fish (then of the University of California) has studied pieces of literature from the perspective of the reader's experience. He operates on the thesis that "meaning is an event, something that happens, not on the page, where we are accustomed to look for it, but in the interaction between the flow of print (or sound) and in the actively mediating consciousness of a reader-hearer."[7] With this thesis he has examined Augustine's answer to the question of what makes good preaching. In the development of his answer Augustine offers several characteristics of good preaching, but as he discusses each one he takes it away and finally treats all he has been saying as irrelevant—God himself is the persuader in good preaching.[8] Notice that what we have is not a truth statement with all portions of the discussion developing that statement. Instead, Augustine leads the reader through an experience of considering and rejecting, as though bridges were being burned behind the traveler through the pages until finally all is consumed except the destination. This focus on the reader puts the writer in the role of narrator, making possible a certain movement for the reader who is overhearing Augustine talk to himself, entertaining and then rejecting his own thoughts. The reader begins to do the same, and the writer's experience is reproduced in the reader.

Professor Fish does a detailed examination of *Paradise Lost* from the perspective of what happens to the reader. *Paradise Lost* is not presented, says Fish, as rhetoric in which the reader accepts or rejects the presentation and its conclusions with no alternatives offered. Rather, *Paradise Lost* is a dialectic in which the reader must arrive at truth. The reader is not so much taught as entangled. How is this done? Here is a lengthy poem about the fall of humanity. The distance between Adam and the present reader, between Paradise and seventeenth-century England, is there to allow freedom to read, relax, agree, disagree, enjoy, or be bored. But the story of Adam is the outer form, and of this form the reader is observer, overhearing the characters as they develop and move through the story. But the inner form is the experience of the reader, for what Milton wanted to do was to make the reader aware of his or her own condition, and seeing corruption, be educated in how to change. The movement follows Plato's dialectic: healthy perplexity, refinement of the eye in discerning one's own progress, and finally the vision of the Supreme Good. Through a long process of travail the reader begins to bridge the distance and participate. Satan is portrayed as attractive, then Milton intrudes himself to warn the reader; and then Satan is again attractive, and further warnings follow. The warnings are overdone and too frequent: The reader sides with Satan *against Milton*, "the preacher." The reader begins to doubt and question her own responses. The outer form falls away like scaffolding as the inner form of the reader's experience develops.

If Professor Fish is right, Milton has not structured a statement to let the reader know where Milton stands on creation, sin, freedom, and salvation. Of course, these are in the poem for any reader who chooses to keep a distance, but the informational dimension of the poem serves another purpose: the conversion of the reader.

This is what I mean by the sacrifice of a communicator in the service of the listener. Certainly some readers or listeners will determine to remain afar off: analyzing, agreeing, disagreeing with the outer form (distance), but never being entangled by the inner form (participation). That is a risk run by the communicator after this fashion. If my ego refuses to allow me to be a communicator in the service of the listener's experience, the outer form will be central, sprinkled, to be sure, with exhortations and applications (after all, I *am* preaching), and the rhetoric will please many but alter few. So also in the classroom: The professor will try for a good lecture, and the student will try for good notes. But suppose now and then, with care and discrimination, a lecture or sermon is framed so as to be a sacrifice, consumed in the process of the listener's being launched in a new direction, provoked or stirred to a new angle of vision. Some will say perhaps it was not as scholarly or as logical or maybe not as good a speech. It may even happen that a student will complain that the form of it or the delivery of it made taking notes more difficult. The ego will flinch, and the speaker will be tempted to leave dialectic (They did not like it.) and return to rhetoric (Many are encouraging me to publish.)

> There was a certain disciple who enrolled in a course offered by the rabbi. The disciple sat before the rabbi with a sheet of paper on which was written only his name. The rabbi began to speak, and the disciple took notes. In addition, the disciple read many books and, as he had been taught, took many notes. It came to pass, however, that as the course progressed the disciple discovered that the increase of his notes did not bring increase of understanding. He stopped taking notes. In fact, he began

to throw away the notes he had. On the last day of class he sat before the rabbi with a sheet of paper on which was written only his name. The disciple complained, "I have nothing to show for my investment of time and money." The rabbi replied, "Do you not understand? This course is a parable."

A third and final suggestion has to do with the structure or stylistic form of the communication. After all, if one is concerned not just with what the message is about but with what is happening to the hearer, the shape of the message is a fundamental consideration. If Stanley Fish is correct, Augustine did not just answer the question, What is good preaching? but he shaped his answer to move the reader from one perspective to another. Similarly, Milton did not write on the fall of humanity simply in order to "justify the ways of God" in a doctrinal sense, but he structured his poem to move, to change the reader. Since communicating can *do* things in the process of speaking-hearing, choosing a stylistic form for effecting the experience is no secondary decision. In other words, good literature *works;* it moves the reader through changes that qualify a person to think, feel, act in new ways. Such is the nature of scripture: The text is productive, generating new levels and directions of life and thought. If the lecture or sermon is to continue that quality, attention must be given to form.

Of course, within any given structure there are many literary aids for enabling the immediates of the speaker to become the immediates of the listener. Even though our society is often characterized as empiricist and scientific, individuals and groups still live in large measure by dreams, images, symbols, and myths. Teaching and preaching that stay in the conceptual world of ideas and doctrines, however true or right or current, leave hearers essentially unmoved. The consciousness in its imaginative depths is unaltered. It is quite often the case that a listener or reader will agree rationally with a position presented with no evidence of modified behavior. The head says yes, but the images of the way life is, or people are, or I am, still hang as they were in the heart's gallery. Many young preachers shake their heads in unbelief when prejudice, greed, sensuality, or social indifference continue unabated even though, says the preacher, "They seemed to agree with the idea I presented." When new images move against the old and shake them into discomfort, then begins painful change. But the longest trip a person ever makes is that from head to heart. This, from the standpoint of effective communication, is a basic flaw in the scheme of Rudolf Bultmann to interpret the New Testament without mythology. "Modern man" is not without mythology. I am convinced that this need for imaginative depth also lies behind much of the increased demand of late for more Bible in the teaching and preaching of the church. There is more here than the stubborn residue of precritical fundamentalism. The language of the Bible—symbolic, dramatic, and imaginative— makes contact with the mythic and poetic consciousness of the readers and hearers.

Among the aids for generating listener experience, perhaps none is more effective than the metaphor. A metaphor is not simply a way of prettifying what is already known, but is a medium of knowing more fully. The metaphor thus sets up a tension that can give a fresh new vision of that which had become familiar. Of course, some object to metaphors as imprecise, dishonest, and self-indulgent. For instance, why not clearly and directly say "the clouds are gray" instead of describing the clouds as sad? Metaphors are necessary in preaching, because a major function of language is to evoke, to draw the mind to the limits of the known, to hold the world before the eye at a new angle, to offer new configurations that shatter old calculations. The use of metaphor is for the communicator an act of creative imagination that has its completion in the equally creative and imaginative act of hearing the metaphor. At the heart of the parables of Jesus is the metaphor.

But imaginative language without a carefully chosen structure that it serves may be little more than teasing and dancing before the listeners. The shape of the communication is paramount in the business of effecting listener experience, and if the experience being sought is overhearing, the structure most congenial and with greatest potential for effectiveness is narrative. Before a narrative the hearer's posture is naturally that of the overhearer. A narrative is told with distance, and sustains it in that the story unfolds on its own, seemingly only casually aware of the hearer, and yet all the while the narrative is inviting and beckoning the listener to participation in its anticipation, struggle, and resolution.

However, so much has been written and said in recent years about "narrative" and "story" in theological discourse that I feel it important to clarify what I do not mean and what I do mean by narrative structure for generating the dynamic of overhearing. First, I do not mean that narrative is to replace rational argument in Christian discourse. Rational argument serves to keep the communication self-critical, athletically trim, and free of a sloppy sentimentality that can take over in the absence of critical activity. We need always to be warned against using narratives and stories to avoid the issues of doctrine, history, and theological reflection. In the church we are doing more than telling anecdotes and sharing illustrations. Some readers of Kierkegaard become enamored of his stories and forget his insistence that Christianity can be conceptualized and that there are times and arenas in which that is the proper business. Nevertheless, it would be fatal for the cause of the gospel to allow *logos* (argument and proof) to discredit the story simply because our culture considers a story to be unscientific. Wherever the narrative is outlawed by theology as precritical, theology becomes an exercise in trading symbols and terms, no longer nourished by experience. And if theology does not reflect critically on human experiences with a view to changing or modifying them, what then does it do?

Second, I do not mean by proposing narrative form that the communicator is to do exegesis and interpretation in the texts of secular literature, ferreting out religious meanings that would justify using these pieces as the substance of Christian communications. There is, no doubt, great value in exploring the explicit and implicit dialogues between the Christian tradition and the secular literature of a given period, but there is something second-rate about combing through this literature for Christian meanings. It often represents a reaction against or an early abandoning of the texts of the Christian faith in favor of impoverishing and depleting the rich world of literature for "relevant" ideas. Many of us are weary of meanings and interpretation that tame art by reducing it to content and then applying the content. Just leave me alone with the narratives to overhear them and to allow them and me room to maneuver. And this includes the narratives of the Bible.

Third, I do not mean by narrative structure that the lecture or sermon consists merely of reading or reciting long narrative portions of scripture verbatim, as though the ancient texts can be thus simply and uncritically transferred from one language, land, culture, and century, to another. The biblical text is always carried through history on the lap of the church, and it is the church's task, through the Holy Spirit, to keep the voice of scripture a living voice through its teaching and preaching. But having said that, let me urge the irreplaceable value, for speaker and listener, of direct exposure to the text. Paul Ricoeur has written perceptively of the value of a naïve reading of the text, allowing the text to touch all our faculties and instincts. Such a reading should be followed by critical examination of the text without fear or reservation. Finally, the student returns to the text with a second naïvete, recovering again the narrative and discourse nature of the text. And even before Ricoeur, Kierkegaard had urged a threefold method: spontaneity, reflection, spontaneity.

Finally, by narrative structure I am not proposing that the lecture or sermon be a long story or a series of stories or illustrations. While such may actually be the form used for a given message, it is not necessary in order for the message to be narrative. Communication may be narrativelike and yet contain a rich variety of materials: poetry, polemic anecdote, humor, exegetical analysis, commentary. To be narrativelike means to have the scope that ties it to the life of a larger community; it means the message has memory and hope; it means to be life-size in the sense of touching all the keys on the board rather than only intellectual or emotional or volitional; it means conveying the sense of movement *from* one place *to* another; it means having this movement on its own, as though the presence of the listeners were not essential to its process; it means thinking alongside the hearers.

Narratives do not summarize events and relationships with commentary and application following. No listeners overhear that. Narratives reproduce and recreate events, with characters developing and events unfolding, and the teller reexperiencing while narrating. This reexperiencing is the source of the emotive and imaginative power in the telling. Emotion and imagination are not added as though options on the part of the speaker. In addition, narratives move from beginning to end, not vice versa for the benefit of lazy ears that want to be sure of the speaker's position, that want to be secure about "where he comes out" but that do not want to have to listen to the message to ascertain it. And finally, narratives move at a pace that most accurately recreates the pace of that which is narrated, sometimes slow, sometimes fast, now meandering, now running.

I pause here to remind myself how difficult it is to do what I have described in the last few sentences. For example, it is not easy to share with listeners the story of Abraham's offering of

Isaac without rushing to the part about the ram caught in the bush. Kierkegaard often complained that preachers would hurry to the happy fact of the ram in the bush or begin with it to assure the anxious or interrupt themselves often to promise the hearers that there will be a ram in the bush soon! Of course, we know the story ended thus, but if the ending is allowed to scatter its smile back over the long and tortuous path of Abraham, his faith is no longer seen as faith; it has been robbed of fear and trembling and is far removed from the pilgrimage of the hearer. A narrative that reproduces the painful journey up Mount Moriah reexperiences all the churning chemistry of a faith that is absolute in its obedience. And those who overhear the story begin to wish for and to despair of, to want and to dread, to seek and to fear finding such faith. These can then enter into Abraham's profound joy and gratitude when the ram appears in the story.

In the same fashion, Easter can abort genuine appreciation of the pilgrimage of Jesus or any real grasp of what it means to follow Jesus. Of course, Easter is there, and from that experience early Christians remembered and anticipated. But introduced too soon into the narrative, and too easily, Easter can make Jesus' ministry a walk-through rehearsal, script in hand, and can make discipleship a real winner. I have heard pastors at funerals make the bereaved feel guilty for their tears. "Don't you believe in the resurrection?" Unfeeling chatter! Easter is *for* the tearful. The Christian faith insists the resurrection perpetuated the nail prints; it did not erase them. Easter has been put too soon in the story from many pulpits with the result that the tomb was not a cave, but a short tunnel. In many churches Easter celebrations are empty of meaning because no one really was dead. The problem? The narrative is lost. In her wisdom the historic church insisted on the narrative: suffering, Good Friday, Easter, waiting, Pentecost. But what if Good Friday services are dropped because they are not successful, and Pentecost is dropped because it comes so late, after school is out and vacations have begun? I know—we can make up for it by having three services on Easter. No—the story has been lost. I go a-fishing.

Probably one reason people will overhear a story with more sustained attention than they will give to many lectures and sermons obviously prepared for them and addressed to them is that a narrative is of the nature of life itself. The form fits. All traditional societies have community stories in which the people live and with which they explain to themselves and to one another their social and metaphysical relationships. The chronology of a narrative locates the participants in time and place. Stories are read and heard because the experience of movement through time, common to the story and all its hearers, reassures that we are alive and can enlarge our living by identifying, participating, and appropriating the experiences of others. This is true even if the narrative disturbs and shocks. And if someone tells me a story large enough, with enough memory and enough hope to provide a context for my own personal narrative, then I am interested.

And this is the story Christians tell. It is very important that the structure of the message be a narrative. A narrative, by its structure, provides order and meaning, and therefore I cannot stress too heavily the indispensability of narrative shape and sequence. Change the shape, for instance, into a logical syllogism, and the question of whether the *content* of the message is altered is a moot one; the important point is the *function* of the message as narrative is now lost. The movement from chaos to order, from origin to destiny, is broken, and in its place are some ideas, well argued.

Again, let the scriptures provide some models. Treat yourself to the experience of reading Mark in a single sitting. Let the narrative form of the gospel move you along through meaningful activity, to crisis, through death, into an open future. Or the book of Acts: Its impact is not solely in its message but in the form of its message. Casting the message as history puts the reader in touch with purposeful struggle toward a future that is God's. In fact, a narrative tends to *do* what it *tells*, mediating suffering and healing and salvation. These values accrue, not in a discussion about the story outside the narrative process, but in the actual telling. Is it too far afield to suggest that some of the efficacy of the Lord's supper lies in the fact that the sacrament is set in a story beginning with the Passover in Egypt and continuing "until he comes," a story into which the life of each participant is placed? "We were in Egypt..." And what was Paul's mission to the Gentiles but a bringing them into the story? His words for it were: adopted, grafted in, children of Abraham by faith, members of the same household. To be a Christian is to have a past as well as a future.

And because in overhearing the story there is not only participation but distance, we are able to endure it. Without the mediating distance of a narrative, there would be something here too wonderful, too fascinating, too dreadful for our capacity to experience. For the awesome claim of the story is that the central character is God. Only indirectly have we seen: Moses coming down from the mountain, his face veiled; He who was in the bosom of the Father, veiled in flesh. And only indirectly have we heard: teachers in the classroom, preachers in the pulpit. All gave the report, veiled in a story.

> *There is no lack of information in a Christian land;*
> *something else is lacking, and this is a something which the*
> *one cannot directly communicate to the other.*

Part III

Sermons

8

"Don't Be Afraid"
(Matthew 28:1–10)[1]

Jesus was dead to begin with. That's hard to pronounce, of course. It's even harder to believe. There are some people you cannot imagine dying. They're so important to so many people that they should not die. It's hard to imagine the world going on without them. Jesus is that person. The one person who never gossiped or criticized or turned his back on anyone, who was tender and gentle and caring and helping to everybody. The one person who made no distinction as to whether you're rich or poor or educated or not. He had a tender care that no one be lost. It's almost impossible to imagine the world without him. Some of us can die and little notice is made of it. We poke around and do so little. Someone says, "You know so-and-so died?" And someone responds, "Well, how did you know? You couldn't tell the difference." But in this case, you could tell the difference. It's so difficult to believe that it's easier just to go into denial about the death of Jesus. And quite early in the history of the church, stories began to circulate that he never really did die. One of the stories went like this:

Do you remember when Jesus was carrying the cross up the hill, and he fell beneath the cross, and they took a man from the crowd called Simon of Cyrene from North Africa? And Simon of Cyrene, he carried the cross. Well, according to this story, when they reached the place of crucifixion, the Roman soldiers didn't know one Jew from the other, and they crucified Simon. Jesus...Jesus didn't die!

Another story that later on became popular was called the Passover Plot. Some of Jesus' followers conspired at the time of his crucifixion. When there was vinegar or sour wine passed to him on a sponge while he was on the cross, they were going to put some strong potion in the sponge, and Jesus would take it, and shortly thereafter his heartbeat and pulse would be reduced so much, hardly perceptible, that the Romans would think he was dead, take him from the cross, put him in the tomb, and then when it wore off, he would come out of the tomb. He never died!

Well the point is, Jesus is dead. We can ask his mother. "Yes. Yes, he's dead." We can ask the soldiers. "Yeah, I was on crucifixion detail, and uh...he's dead!" Go ask his followers. They all abandoned him and ran. Unbelievable. Unbelievable! After all that time with him, and in his hour of crisis, they ran. Oh, they were all glad to be in the group in Galilee, and they were just having such a wonderful time in huge crowds—approving crowds—you call the roll: "Matthew? Here. Judas? Here. Peter? Here! Simon? Here! James? Here! John? Here." Everyone! Perfect attendance! "We're Jesus' friends, you know. We follow Jesus. We're the Jesus people. They call us Nazarenes. We're with Jesus. We're with Jesus." Then, when the Galilean spring is over and the Jerusalem winter sets in, it's no longer a matter of watching Jesus, but a matter of saying, "He's gone, we'll have to do it ourselves! We're going to have to work harder, give more, serve more!" Whew! Matthew? He's not here. He's back collecting taxes. James and John? They're not here. They're fishing with their dad again. Where are they?

Forever after when they returned to preaching, one little part of their sermon was missing, and that was in response to the question, "Were you there when they crucified him?" No. Don't ask them. Ask the women from Galilee. Oh, they came in great numbers, and they followed him, helpless as they were, watching everything. Jesus turned to them and said, "Women, don't cry for me. Cry for yourselves. This is a terrible time. And if they'll do this while the wood is green, just think what they'll do when it's dry! It's going to be hard on you!" But they were there. They were faithful. Especially the two Marys mentioned in our text—Mary Magdelene and Mary the mother of James and Joseph. There were a lot of Marys in the New Testament. But they were all named after that one grand lady of the Old Testament: Miriam, the sister of Moses. A very popular name. These two Marys came. They came into the place, the cemetery. They returned to the cemetery. You know what that is like, don't you? Returning to the cemetery after everybody's gone? I think we took my mother back four times. I wanted to go back out to the cemetery. Luke says they came to anoint the body, but not in Matthew! That's already been done!

What are these women doing? They come up the hill and are absolutely shocked to find a detachment of Roman soldiers. "What are you doing here? Guarding a dead man? Boy, this must be the crack troops of the Emperor guarding a dead man."

"Oh, be quiet. We didn't ask for this duty. We have this thing marked off like a crime scene."

"Well, the crime has already been committed. Why are you doing this? He's dead. Aren't you satisfied?"

"Now go along, women. Leave us alone. We've been told in the street that some of his followers might come in here at night, steal the body, then go up and down the towns saying, 'He's risen! He's risen! He's risen!' We're not going to let that happen. What are you women doing here?"

"Well, we're friends of the deceased."

"Then why did you come out here?"

Good question. Why did they go back to the cemetery? We don't know. But we can imagine why we would do it. You're away from people. You can think. Kind of rehash in our minds what happened. See if we can understand it. Get a little closure, maybe, on this terrible thing. "We don't know why we came. It's just that we were sitting at the house, and it just seemed somehow, unfeeling, and thoughtless, and not caring to be sitting at the house when Jesus was out here—we...we just came."

And it was while they were sitting there that this extraordinary thing happened. The four gospel writers tell about it in a different way, because how can you describe what can't be described? There was this enormous...enormous moment of divine revelation and visitation, and a messenger from heaven said, "He's not here! Look in the grave! He's gone! He's not here. He's risen just as he said!" And they looked in. He wasn't there! And the messenger said, "Now you go tell his disciples." They ran from the tomb, and on the way, they met Jesus, and they worshiped him. He said, "Wait, Women! Go and tell my brothers I will meet them in Galilee just as I told them. Now run along. Run along!" And they did.

Now I want you to know a couple of things that Matthew tells us in this brief account. Just a couple of things.

First, Matthew says that the people who first experienced the risen Christ were the ones that were there for the funeral. Let it soak in. You don't skip from Palm Sunday to Easter! There's Maundy Thursday, the last meal. There's Good Friday, the last hours. Then there's Easter. Friends, you cannot have enough flowers. You can't have enough new clothes. You can't have enough visitors. You can't have enough choir anthems and sermons and scripture and anything else to make up for the fact that if I wasn't there at Good Friday, how can it be Easter? I don't understand it. I frankly do not understand how people can expect so much from Easter when they didn't even go to the funeral. These women were there. They watched him die. They watched him get buried. And then they came back. I don't know where you were on Good Friday. Some of you were out shopping. Some of you were in your own homes reflecting on the death of Jesus. Some of you were in Good Friday services somewhere. You know what I'd like to think? Can I think this just for a moment? It may not be true, but let me think it—that everybody in this room on Friday experienced Good Friday. That qualifies you for Easter.

The second thing Matthew says—I hope you didn't miss it—is that when the women were on their way, they met Christ and worshiped him, experienced him, and he said, "Get on now! Go on your mission!" When did they meet the living Christ? While they were doing what the messenger told. While they were on a mission. While they were doing his work they had the experience. You know a lot of people say to me, "Do you have a book to suggest that will help me to have a little spiritual experience in Christ and everything?" I don't have a book. I just have an assignment. Do something for somebody, and in the process of doing what Jesus did, carrying on what he did, you will have some marvelous experiences. Talk to people who serve food at the community food pantry, and they'll tell you there are some Wednesdays when they're passing out peanut butter and canned potatoes that it's more Sunday than Sunday.

At the clothes closet here, you talk to those people who work through those clothes. That's a tough job! Some of those clothes smell bad, and we have to burn them. They're not good for anybody. You just emptied your closet—thanks anyway! But some of them are good enough for somebody. And you watch kids rifle through there and find a shirt or maybe find a dress. And the people who work at the clothes closet will tell you that Thursday afternoon is more Sunday than Sunday.

There's not a book that's going to do it. There is an assignment that's going to do it. It was in the process of doing what he wanted done that they experienced Christ. Twice to the women it was said, "Don't be afraid. Don't be afraid." I don't know if it worked or not. It's easy to say, "Don't be afraid." That's the end of the gospel. That is the gospel.

You remember how it all started? Not long ago, we were reading those texts. Seems like just a little while ago. And while shepherds were watching their flocks at night, an angel appeared and said, "Don't be afraid. I have good news of great joy for everybody." You remember? Not long ago. Do you remember how it started? Mary in Nazareth of Galilee, and Gabriel said, "Now, Mary, Mary, Mary! Don't be afraid. God has chosen you." Do you remember Joseph? Do you remember how it started? Joseph had a dream, and in this dream the voice said, "Don't be afraid, Joseph, to take Mary as your wife. This is God's doing." He started to be afraid. "Don't be afraid. Don't be afraid." And it ends with "Don't be afraid. Don't be afraid. Don't be afraid."

You see, the opposite of faith is fear. Fear is death itself.

"Why don't you go out for the ball team?" "I'm afraid I won't make it."

"Why don't you try out for the school play?" "I'm afraid I won't get a part."

"Why did you lie to your parents?" "I was afraid of punishment."

"Why did you cheat on the test?" "I was afraid I would fail."

"Why were you so jealous?" "I was afraid of losing love."

"Why did you cling so tightly to your purse?" "I was afraid of insecurity."

Afraid, afraid, afraid, afraid, afraid, afraid. That's the refrain of what we are and do. But don't be afraid. Don't be afraid to live and love and laugh. Don't be afraid to give and serve and care. Don't be afraid to speak and do. That's the message of Easter. Don't be afraid. For he said, "I'll be with you. Always. Even to the end of the world." That's Easter. Amen.

9

"The Bottom Line" (Matthew 7:21–29)

This is the ending of the Sermon on the Mount. The Sermon on the Mount occupies Matthew 5, 6, and 7, and we have just heard the close of the matter. That's important to know in understanding what is being said. Those of you who've been taught something in public speaking or communication know the principle of "end stress"—that what is said at the very end is usually the most important thing. I've tried to teach that to my students in preaching classes, once in a while with success, but not usually, because the temptation is to start your preparation with the front of the sermon, the beginning of the sermon, and work through. The proper way is to start with a conclusion and work back. If you start at the first, you put all your best thought and energy into the first part of it, and by the time you get to the end, it's just kind of a whimper or a trickle, trailing on in mere repetition. No—start at the end and move forward. Edgar Allen Poe described how he wrote his poem *The Raven*. He said, "I wrote the closing two stanzas first. And then I wrote stanzas that would take me to that point." He didn't begin "Once upon a midnight dreary." He ended there. You don't build the porch first. You build the porch after you have a house to which it's built. It's important to know that this text is the end of the Sermon on the Mount.

The Sermon on the Mount given to us by Matthew—a collection of the teachings of Jesus on matters relational, ethical, personal, communal—begins with the Beatitudes. "Blessed are the humble, the meek, the poor in spirit, the peacemakers, those who hunger and thirst for righteousness." And from the Beatitudes begins the instruction. Whatever you do, you do before other people; therefore, your behavior is extremely important. Jesus talked about relationships. Primary relationships. Even if you're at the altar giving your gift, and you remember that a brother or sister has something against you, leave your gift and go take care of it because that's so, so important. He talked about telling the truth. He talked of marriage and divorce. He talked about how to deal with those who hate you, those who are opposed to you, how to turn the other cheek, how to go the second mile. He talked about not judging. He talked about prayer. And he gave us the Lord's Prayer in chapter 6. He talked about giving alms for the poor. He talked about not being ensnared in things, worrying about what we should eat, what we should drink, what we should wear. You seek first the kingdom of God and God's righteousness. You'll have these other things. He talked about so many things that have to do with how we behave. And at the end of it, he said, "Not everybody who says Lord, Lord, will enter the kingdom of heaven." There'll be on that day people who come and say, "Lord, Lord, didn't we in your name preach?" *Yes.* "Didn't we in your name do miracles?" *Yes.* "Didn't we in your name cast out demons?" *Yes.* "Well, then, let us in." *Get out of here, I don't even know who you are.* Mmm! He said, "Whoever hears these words and does them is like a person who builds the house on the rock. And whenever the storm comes, it'll hold. But if you hear these words of mine and don't do them, you build a beautiful home on sand. And when the storm comes, the home is gone." And the people were absolutely amazed at his teaching because of his authority.

The word *authority* in the New Testament is a word that simply means, "from out of yourself." *Exousia.* He spoke out of himself! He didn't just speak what other people said, quote a lot of other people. He spoke out of his own character. And they were flabbergasted. That's a powerful ending to the Sermon on the Mount.

The second principle—you don't mind a little class in preaching do you?—the second principle is: Always end on a positive note. Always end with some good news. You don't just turn down the mouth and the voice, give a word of warning, uncap hell and shake people over it, then have a benediction! Have some good news of God's love and grace! That's the note on which you end! And so we look at the closing of the Sermon on the Mount, and it is not there. "Not everybody who says 'Lord, Lord'"... because talking religion is absolutely no substitute for what I have been teaching you. "But we preached!" *Yeah.* "We did a lot of harmless things! We gave big gifts! We did some attention-getting work in your name!" *That's true.* "Then what's the problem?" Nothing is a substitute for doing what is right. The ethically right thing to do. That's fundamental. And then he gives a parable of the house on the rock and the house on the sand. Which comes last? Sand! "And great was the fall of it." Now why does he do that? Why would anybody go contrary to the fundamental principle of ending on a positive note?

Well, there could be several reasons. One is that whenever a group of listeners or readers face a danger to the soul, a danger to the spirit, a danger to one's salvation that is so seductive, so persuasive, so powerful, so dangerous, you just have to scream: "Warning! Watch out!" What will happen? How many parents on the day the youngster gets the driver's license take them down to the highway patrol office to look at the big black-and-white, blown-up photographs of twisted steel, broken glass, and blood on the pavement? Not trying to end on a negative note, but making an impression. It's this important; it's this serious. Maybe that's the reason.

You know what I think the reason is? I think Jesus is trying to impress upon them in this very dramatic, intimidating, almost frightening talk that what he's talking about is difficult. You love your enemies. How's that for a starter? Go a second mile if somebody forces you to go one. If someone takes you to court and wants your overcoat, give them your shirt too. Mmm! For starters, how often shall we forgive? Seventy times seven? Whew! The difficulty, the difficulty for the sincere—now I'm talking to the sincere—the difficulty for the sincere and conscientious follower of Jesus is that the Christian life has tensions built into it, and there is no simple resolution. Paul said it himself long after he was converted, years after he was converted, years after he had been a missionary and preacher and apostle. "I don't understand my own actions. In my mind I serve God. But there is another force at work in my life. I don't understand it. And while I want to do what is right, I don't do it. When I want to avoid what is wrong, I still do it. I am stretched between the two. Here is my intention. Here is my performance. God, who will deliver me?" It's built into the nature of the case, and no living, breathing human being ever resolves it short of death. As long as you have imagination and fire and anger, and get hurt and mistreated and oppressed, then something is going to rear up that is against the teaching of Jesus. But it's there! It's there! Some people would rather solve it by just having nothing to do with the body and things of this world. And they don't hit a lick for anybody; they don't do anything. They don't show up for work day at church; they don't take any food to anyone. They don't volunteer for the food pantry, the clothes closet. They don't do anything. "I'm just trying to keep my soul pure. And the best way to do that is to avoid you people." No, that won't resolve it! And some people resolve it by just attending to the physical—the fleshly—and pay no attention to the spirit. And did you know that you could do that? You could avoid God's people, avoid the Bible, avoid prayer, avoid work day, avoid Christian gatherings, avoid all that, and I think over a period of time, you would be like a cow or an ox or a jackass. Sunday is the same as every other day. Possible. And then the tension is gone.

The tension is built in me. And the Christian life is a struggle. It's not simple. You don't just put something on a bumper sticker: "God said it, I believe it, and that's it." Well, that looks good on the bumper. But nobody—nobody—nobody lives that simply. It's built into our families. The expression used commonly is "cycles." People, children, get in cycles depending on the family, the extended family, and the community, and you get into that cycle. We speak of cycles of violence, cycles of poverty, cycles of prejudice. There are also cycles of greed, cycles of arrogance, cycles of superiority. And these family members and these friends have powerful influence. How do you break it? Every time—every time—every time there is a child that shows up to church alone, *Where's your mother?* "She doesn't come." *Where's your father?* "He doesn't come." *Are they going to come with you some time?* "No. I get a ride with a neighbor who comes." What chance does the child have? We can love, we can pray, we can care, and once in a while...once in a while. But usually, it's that cycle. Early pregnancy. Alcohol. Prejudice. Violence. How do you break it? The reason it's so hard to break is because the people you love and the people who love you don't want you to break it.

When Clyde—I'll just use his first name—walked out of a little coal-mining village in southwest Virginia with all his possessions in a gunnysack, he was leaving. He was in a family of fourteen children. He had already started going to the mine, at fourteen years old. And a teacher—a teacher—in the grade school said, "Do you want some more books to read at night?" *Yes!* "At the end of grade school, would you like to go on to high school?" *Oh no, I'll have to go on to work. Everybody else in the family...* "But wouldn't you like to go on?" He did. And then high school. And then the same teacher said, "College? Would you like to go to college?" Clyde walked to the highway, everything in that gunnysack, and caught a bus to college. I asked him one day, I said, "Clyde, what was the hardest part of that?" He said, "It was not the poverty. It was not missing my family or missing my home. The hardest part was everybody who loved me said, 'Don't leave. Why are you running away? Don't leave us with all the work to do. You're betraying us.'" And he said that hurt. "Why not just stay here, stay here, stay here; these people love you."

Then Sam showed up in high school, poor as Job's turkey. Couldn't buy his own lunch. Principal said, "Well, we'll give you lunch. But we'd like for you to do a little work around here." So Sam swept the hallways, sometimes ran the mop over the gymnasium floor, sometimes put a little coal in the furnace to keep the fire going. But the jobs began to multiply. And they let him out of third period, and let him out of fifth period, and let him out of sixth period. He worked through lunch. And pretty soon he was around the school, but he was not in school. He was working for the school, and he got his lunch, and when he was almost seventeen he quit. And now he's married. He's not a carpenter, but he can help a carpenter. He's not a mechanic, but he can help a mechanic. He doesn't have any real skills. He has a wife. He has four children. He makes minimum wage—nothing wrong with that. Except a school, a school made it impossible for him to ever look in a microscope and see a world you could never see with the eye, made it impossible for him to look in a telescope and see the world—the universe. He never turned the pages of great books of poetry, and literature, and drama. He was never introduced to a map of the world. He was pushing a broom, and they gave him his lunch. And he was thus treated by people in his own community, his own school, his own friends and relatives, so that the world was closed off and the cycle continued. Criminal activity!

I don't know. I think Jesus speaks this alarming language because there is—let's face it, let's just be honest—there is built into the nature of Christian living every day some tension. Right now in the world, tension exists between justice and forgiveness. How can we have justice for people who've been hurt and oppressed and mistreated, and forgive and love and embrace the people who oppress and hurt? The Bible says and Jesus says, "Do both." How can I do both? And there are fifty wars going on right now in the world, and almost every one of them is simply this: "Well, we've got to punish." *But shouldn't we forgive?* "Oh, you're a bunch of those lily-livered liberals. Always talking about love and forgiveness." *Well you're those cold, cruel, heartless people who want to get even.* What's the resolution? The tragedy is—the tragedy is—that in most of those fifty wars in the world right now, religion is being called on to sanction the effort. Come on! Let's get with it!

I notice where Miroslav Volf, who's a Croatian, wrote recently about going back to his country. It used to be Yugoslavia; now it's Croatia and Serbia. And he went back to his home to visit his family and his friends in Croatia, and he enjoyed it, and he began to ask about some Serbs. "Well, well, they're not with us anymore." *But we played ball together. We used to shoot hoops out back of the school together.* "Oh, well some of them are dead." *What?!?* "Why are you asking about the Serbs? You're a Croatian." *Well, they're friends of mine.* "They're not!" And you know what he said? "They wanted me to be so loyal to Croatia that I proved it by hating everybody else. And you know what I am if I don't do that? I'm not a loyal citizen. I'm not patriotic." And he said, "I could not do it."

That's what we're being asked to do. "What's the matter with you? Are you weak? Are you a compromiser? What do you mean loving and forgiving? Stand for what's right!" As for myself—as for myself—I refuse to allow my religion to be used in the service of anything less than God. But sometimes duty seems to demand a hammer of justice. So what do I do? This is right: We have to have justice. This is right: We're to love and forgive the unjust. How can I live this way? No wonder Jesus gave such a dramatic, outstanding, and shocking conclusion to the Sermon. You will have this struggle as long as you live. Don't let anyone solve it by just saying, "Love and forgive." Or by just saying, "Take up your guns!" I have to live here. And where is here?

Sometimes I say, "God, be merciful to me, a sinner." Sometimes I say, "Who's going to deliver me from this tension, this anxiety, this struggle?" Thanks be to God for God's love in Jesus Christ. Most of the time I stand in the Sermon on the Mount when Jesus says—you remember, right at the beginning he said—"My blessing, my blessing on those who are hungry and thirsty for what is right!" That's the bottom line. Amen.

10

"Old Story, New Ending" (Luke 16:19–31)

Probably no two characters have caught the imagination or stirred the emotions of people more than the characters in this story. It is a story told by Jesus according to Luke. It's about a rich man who is nameless. In the Latin translation, "rich" is *dives,* and so he's called *Dives.* He has no name. And there's a beggar at his gate named Lazarus. Both these men stir deep emotions in us. The rich man does. He is for many people the envy of their lives. His big home. Well appointed. Comfortable. They try to get him to put it on the big parade of homes each year so people can see inside. But he refuses. It's his house, with a banquet table set every day for him, fine clothes every time he goes out on the street. Imported fabric. Purple and fine linen. I don't know if you realize it, but there are a lot of young people in college today who take him as the picture of success. If I could have that house, those clothes, that income, that banquet table. He stirs a lot of feelings in us. Hatred. He is so cold. So coldhearted and self-centered and greedy.

Of Lazarus, there is nothing to be envied. Everything to be pitied. A wretched creature he is. Only those who look on him with eyes of love and care can see any remnant of the image of God in that poor man. He lies there on the curb, his sunken eyes looking out from their sockets toward the house. The rich man's house. And with weakened voice, "Alms for the poor!" Waiting for that half-biscuit. That uneaten roll. That bone from a rack of lamb. Just anything. But nothing comes. Too weak to stand, he lies at the curb, and the dogs lick his sores. It is he of the two characters that has caught our hearts. And there we hold him. Lazarus the beggar. He's in our music the choir sang. (And quite well, I might say. I'm rather reluctant to say things like that, but, uh—I like that song.) It's in our music. It's in our language: "Poor as Lazarus." We think of Lazarus with his sores when someone gets a bad rash or sores on his skin. Sometimes you hear people say, "I feel like a regular Lazarus." In England, when they started building homes for the poor, they called them Lazarus houses, and everybody knew what they were: poorhouses.

Some people not only feel strongly sympathetic for Lazarus but actually identify with him. Picture yourself going to a little cinder block church. Very crude. The members made it themselves. Nothing ornate; they built the table, built the pulpit, made crude pews, borrowed hymnals. Low income. This little church in the poorer section of town is having a revival. They brought in a fiery preacher from somewhere to stir them up! And they sit there in the heat of the summer evening fanning themselves with those hand fans from Brown Funeral Home, trying to stay alive and awake while the preacher talks to them about the rich man. The preacher identifies and assumes they all identify with Lazarus. And the whole sermon is setting the rich man up on a post like putting a pumpkin up there and then inviting everyone to shoot their poisoned arrows into him—poisoned arrows of envy and bitterness and hatred for all his wealth. The preacher gives voice to how they feel and spends the whole forty-minute sermon attacking the rich man. Ah, the rich man has a patio. And everybody laughs. "Didn't you know he has a patio? Oh, he has a patio! He likes to go out after a big meal and sit on his patio. And he goes out, and there's no patio. God has sent some groundhogs to burrow underneath it, and it's all fallen in." And everybody applauds. "Oh, the rich man has a swimming pool. Did you know he had a swimming pool? He has a swimming pool! Big fence around it in case any of the kids in the neighborhood want to use it. He likes to swim before dinner, work up a good appetite. He goes out to use it, and it's dry as a chip! Because God has sent an angel down to pull the plug, and there's no water." And everybody applauds. "And so the rich man turns to go back in the house, and there's no house because it has turned into a tent and the closet full of clothes is a box of rags, and the roof leaks, and the rent is due, and we say to him, 'Mr. Rich Man, welcome to our world.'" And everybody stood and applauded. Forty minutes of attack on this man. What redemptive exercise there was in this, I don't know. But they went away feeling real good about the attack.

My first recollection of introduction to this text was in church. I was sitting there in the accustomed place with brothers and sister and mother. The service had hardly started, and I was already bored out of my gourd, but I sat there and tried to stay as still as possible. I was paying attention that day because on the pulpit was a white cloth over something. You could tell there was something under the cloth. All through the songs and prayers I awaited it patiently; then the minister got up and read the text from Luke 16. "There was a certain rich man dressed in purple and fine linen who ate a banquet every day. And at his gate sat a poor beggar named Lazarus." And so he read. And when he got to the part where he said, "Father Abraham, send Lazarus back to the earth to warn my brothers so that they will not come to this place of torment," the preacher stopped and said, "What message did he want to send back to his brothers? That's what we want to hear today."

And he lifted the cloth. And under the cloth was a human skull. It scared me to death! My mother told me later he probably got it from a dentist's office. It was a human skull, and the upper jaw and lower jaw were fastened by thick rubber bands, and every time he made a point in the sermon, he would chuck the chin of that thing and the teeth would click. And he would make his point. And as a nine-year-old, I went away from church with one promise: I am not going to torment. That's one thing for sure. I remember it!

By the time I was myself a preacher, I was aware that I and the members of the church I served were not the rich man. We were not the poor man. We were middle class. Middle class. Comfortable, but not rich. Wishing for more, but not Lazarus. And so, since we were in the middle as middle-class Americans, I gave advice to the rich and to the poor. I said to the poor, "Don't be envious. Don't be consumed by envy and bitterness toward those who have more. Don't think that money will solve all your problems. Don't overestimate what it will do for you. Don't spend all your time at the supper table talking in front of your children about, 'If we had this, and if we had that, and if we had something else.' I want to tell you that you can be greedy and poor! It is not money that is the root of all evil. It's the love of money. And you can be broke and love money." That's what I said to the poor. And I gave advice to the rich. "A person's life does not consist of the abundance of what you have. You can be rich in things, but poor in soul. Money is a seductive and deceitful thing and will promise you what money can never give you! Watch it. Watch it. Watch it." That's what I said. But now, as I stand on the summit of my years, I have finally come to understand this story.

This story was told to me. I am the rich man. You didn't know that. I am the rich man. I should explain. We have two vehicles in our house. A car and a utility vehicle. We almost own our home. If things go as they're going now, in the year 2008 we will make the last payment on our home. I am the rich man. I am retired and receive—and in fact it's put directly into the bank—Social Security income. And pension from my years in the ministry. It's put in the bank. Did you know that many months those two together amount to a lot more than we spend? And if it begins to add up, we can do something sort of special. But that's enough. We're on Medicare, and we have supplemental insurance. I'm a rich man!

Now some people say, "Yes! But what about a lengthy illness toward the end of your life? What about catastrophic illness?" Well, I guess I'd do what others do. Sell the house. That would put Nettie and me in a nice sunroom in some place, sitting among a flock of wheelchairs with plastic lilies, large-print Bibles, and old checkerboards. It'll take care of it for quite a while. And when that runs out, and we stay alive, we'll just call the kids and say, "Your turn!" And when that runs out, I will be wheeled into this congregation, and I'll say, "Okay, folks, it's your turn."

I'm the rich man. I am. I'm not playing a trick. I'm telling you the truth. But I made up my mind about this: that I will never lose my soul because I'm rich. I will not do it. I absolutely refuse to lose my soul because I'm a rich man. I want to stay free. As the apostle Paul said to the Philippian church, "I know how to have a lot. I know how to have nothing." My temperature does not go up and down; my mood does not go up and down; my depression does not come when I'm broke. I can be broke. Praise God! I can have a lot. Praise God! I can handle it because I'm free in Jesus Christ and adequate for every circumstance. And I insist on keeping my freedom. I will not lose it to a dollar bill. Never. I've learned some things through the years. I've learned that money does not give you any identity at all. Did you notice—in the text the poor man has a name: Lazarus. The rich man has no name. You think that's accidental? It's not accidental. The point of the story is: He has a big house, he has a lot of food, he has really nice clothes. But what's his name? Apart from his money, he is nobody. What a pitiful, pitiful thing. I've learned some things through the years. I've learned what money will do. It will do a lot. It will give goods and services to folks who need it. It really will. It will lift the quality of life for a lot of people. Just some money will do it. But I know what money will not do. It will not buy a home. A house, sure, but not a home. A companion, yes, but not a friend. A water pipe to your house, yes, but no rain. A fine watch, but no time. A beautiful Bible, but no salvation. I've learned that. I have learned that when somebody in need approaches me, automatically, automatically a part of what I have belongs to that person. And if I don't give it, it is stealing. Because it's not mine anymore. And if I keep it, it's embezzling.

I've learned some things as a rich man. I have learned that you should never compare yourself with anyone else in terms of goods. Anyone below you can make you arrogant. Anyone above you can make you envious. None of that is a good game. That's a fatal game. You don't know how it is with someone else. I believe that there are people to whom God gives the gift to make money, to make a lot of money. And then they have the burden of what to do with it. What to do with it as a believing Christian person. What do I do with it? Prosperity is a cloud over some people, and they would gladly change places with some of us who have a rather simple life. Don't envy anybody. Just no comparing with anybody. Your station in life is a gift of God. I'm telling you the truth. I'm a rich man. I know. I've been hearing it talked about, and I know in November the finance committee of this church is going to present to the congregation for vote a budget that will indicate in terms of dollars and cents the premiums, priorities, and convictions of this church: who is going to be relieved, and helped, and served, and blessed by the money of this church. And they'll present it as a budget. And I'll be asked to say yes or no to that. I know that's going to happen. And if I say yes, I know what's going to happen after that. They're going to come around and say, "Are you going to make a commitment to see that this happens?" That's what they're going to do. And I'm going to do it. I might even—I'm not boasting here—but I might give a little more than we can afford just to make sure that I stay free. I expect this church to hold me accountable as a rich man. Keep my feet to the fire. Set me free. Keep me free. Because I am rich. And I live in the midst of people who are very rich. Amen.

Notes

Chapter 1: Concerning Method

[1]Somerset Maugham, *The Summing Up* (Garden City, N.Y.: Doubleday, 1938), 87–88.

[2]Søren Kierkegaard, *Either/Or*, trans. David and Lillian Swenson (Garden City, N.Y.: Doubleday, 1959), 281.

[3]Maugham, *Summing Up*, 43.

[4]Susan Sontag, *Against Interpretation* (New York: Dew, 1966), 29.

[5]John Dryden, Earl of Roscommon, ed., *Divine Hours and Prayers*, 3d ed. (London: W. Taylor, 1719).

[6]Brian Wicker, *The Story-Shaped World* (Notre Dame, Ind.: University of Notre Dame Press, 1975), 87.

Chapter 2: Concerning the Listener

[1]George Eliot, *Middlemarch* (New York: Houghton Mifflin, 1956), 144.

[2]Søren Kierkegaard, *The Point of View for My Work as an Author*, trans. Walter Lowrie (New York: Harper & Row, 1962), 23–24.

[3]Søren Kierkegaard, *Concluding Unscientific Postscript*, trans. David Swenson and Walter Lowrie (Princeton, N.J.: Princeton University Press, 1941), 519.

[4]Ibid., 327.

[5]Søren Kierkegaard, *The Present Age*, trans. Alexander Dru and Walter Lowrie (London: Oxford University Press, 1940), 11.

[6]Ibid., 1–18.

[7]Paul Holmer, "Kierkegaard and Theology," *Union Seminary Quarterly Review* 12 (1957): 26.

[8]Kierkegaard, *Concluding Unscientific Postscript*, 130.

[9]Ibid., 219–20.

[10]Susan Sontag, *Against Interpretation* (New York: Dew, 1966), 257.

[11]Søren Kierkegaard, *Attack upon "Christendom,"* trans. Walter Lowrie (Princeton, N.J.: Princeton University Press, 1944), 30.

[12]Kierkegaard, *Concluding Unscientific Postscript*, 49.

[13]Kierkegaard, *Point of View*, 24, 30.

[14]Søren Kierkegaard, *Works of Love*, trans. David and Lillian Swenson (Princeton, N.J.: Princeton University Press, 1946), 21.

[15]Kierkegaard, *Attack upon "Christendom,"* 140.

[16]Franz Kafka, *Parables and Paradoxes* (New York: Schocken Books, 1946), 81.

[17]Kierkegaard, *Concluding Unscientific Postscript*, 351.

[18]Paul Holmer, *C. S. Lewis: The Shape of His Faith and Thought* (New York: Harper, 1976), 115.

[19]Kierkegaard, *Concluding Unscientific Postscript*, 147.

[20]Ibid., 261.

[21]Henry Thoreau, "Walden," in *The Work of Thoreau*, ed. H. S. Canby (Boston: Houghton Mifflin, 1937), 255.

[22]George Steiner, *Language and Science* (New York: Atheneum, 1967), 11.

Chapter 3: Concerning the Teller

[1]Søren Kierkegaard, *The Point of View for My Work as an Author*, trans. Walter Lowrie (New York: Harper & Row, 1962), 117.

[2]Walter Slatoff, *With Respect to Readers* (Ithaca, N.Y.: Cornell University Press, 1970), 93–97.

[3]Søren Kierkegaard, *Concluding Unscientific Postscript*, trans. David Swenson and Walter Lowrie (Princeton, N.J.: Princeton University Press, 1941), 365.

[4]Ibid.

[5]Kierkegaard, *Point of View*, 117.

⁶Ibid., 89–90.

⁷Somerset Maugham, *The Summing Up* (Garden City, N.Y.: Doubleday, 1938), 1–7.

⁸Søren Kierkegaard, *Edifying Discourses,* trans. David and Lillian Swenson, 4 vols. (Minneapolis: Augsburg, 1943), 2:54.

⁹Kierkegaard, *Concluding Unscientific Postscript,* 174.

¹⁰Ibid., 31.

¹¹Søren Kierkegaard, *Attack upon "Christendom,"* trans. Walter Lowrie (Princeton, N.J.: Princeton University Press, 1944), 181.

¹²John Updike, "The Fork," in *Kierkegaard: A Collection of Critical Essays,* ed. Josiah Thompson (Garden City, N.Y.: Doubleday, 1972), 170.

¹³Kierkegaard, *Concluding Unscientific Postscript,* 70.

¹⁴Kierkegaard, *Point of View,* 27–28.

¹⁵Ibid., 34.

¹⁶Kierkegaard, *Concluding Unscientific Postscript,* 222.

Chapter 4: Concerning the Story

¹Søren Kierkegaard, *Concluding Unscientific Postscript,* trans. David Swenson and Walter Lowrie (Princeton, N.J.: Princeton University Press, 1941), 339.

²Ibid., 346.

³Søren Kierkegaard, *Journals,* trans. Alexander Dru (New York: Harper, 1959), X1, A, 246.

⁴Ibid., X1, A, 640.

⁵E. Käsemann, "Blind Alleys in the 'Jesus of History' Controversy," in *New Testament Questions of Today,* trans. W. J. Montague (Philadelphia: Fortress Press, 1969), 48.

⁶ Søren Kierkegaard, *On Authority and Revelation,* trans. Walter Lowrie (Princeton, N.J.: Princeton University Press, 1955), 168–69.

⁷Kierkegaard, *Journals,* IX, A, 442.

⁸W. A. Beardslee, *Literary Criticism of the New Testament* (Philadelphia: Fortress Press, 1970), 9.

⁹Robert Funk, *Jesus as Precursor* (Missoula, Mont.: Society of Biblical Literature, 1975), 52.

¹⁰E. D. Hirsch, *Validity in Interpretation* (New Haven, Conn.: Yale University Press, 1967), ix–x.

¹¹James Barr, "Story and History in Biblical Theology," *Journal of Religion* 56 (1976): 16.

¹²Amos Wilder, *Theopoetic* (Philadelphia: Fortress Press, 1976), 27.

¹³Ibid., 84.

¹⁴Paul Holmer, "Theology and Belief," in *Essays on Kierkegaard,* ed. Jerry Gill (Minneapolis: Burgess Publishing, 1969), 1996–97.

¹⁵Roland Barthes, "Science vs. Literature," in *Introduction to Structuralism,* ed. Michael Lane (New York: Basic Books, 1970), 411.

¹⁶Hans Frei, *The Eclipse of Biblical Narrative* (New Haven, Conn.: Yale University Press, 1974), 17.

¹⁷Stephen Crites, "The Narrative Quality of Experience," *Journal of the American Academy of Religion* 39 (1971): 310.

¹⁸Beardslee, *Literary Criticism;* Robert C. Tannehill, *The Sword of His Mouth* (Philadelphia: Fortress Press, 1975).

¹⁹Paul Ricoeur, "Biblical Hermeneutics," *Semeia* 4 (1975): 86.

Chapter 5: By Way of Kierkegaard

¹Søren Kierkegaard, *Journals,* trans. Alexander Dru (New York: Harper, 1959), X2, A, 466.

²Ibid., X3, A, 534.

³E. Schillebeeckx, "The Crisis in the Language of Faith as a Hermeneutical Problem," in *The Crisis of Religious Language,* ed. J. B. Metz and J. P. Jossua (New York: Herder and Herder, 1973), 33.

[4]Kierkegaard, *Journals*, XI2, A, 27.

[5]Søren Kierkegaard, *Concluding Unscientific Postscript*, trans. David Swenson and Walter Lowrie (Princeton, N.J.: Princeton University Press, 1941), 211.

[6]Søren Kierkegaard, *The Point of View for My Work as an Author*, trans. Walter Lowrie (New York: Harper & Row, 1962), 24–25.

[7]Kierkegaard, *Journals*, VIII2, A, 243.

[8]Ibid., X4, A, 317.

[9]Ibid., VII2, A, 362.

[10]Stephen Crites, "Pseudonymous Authorship as Art and as Act," in *Kierkegaard: A Collection of Critical Essays*, ed. Josiah Thompson, Modern Studies in Philosophy 18 (Garden City, N.Y.: Anchor Books, 1972), 228.

[11]Paul Ricoeur, "Biblical Hermeneutics," *Semeia* 4 (1975): 100–106.

[12]Kierkegaard, *Concluding Unscientific Postscript*, 246–47.

[13]Kierkegaard, *Point of View*, 38.

[14]Kierkegaard, *Journals*, VII2, B, 82.

[15]Quoted in Paul Holmer, *C. S. Lewis: The Shape of His Faith and Thought* (New York: Harper, 1976), 4.

[16]Kierkegaard, *Point of View*, 25–26.

[17]Kierkegaard, *Journals*, IX, A, 198.

[18]Ibid., XI2, A, 289.

[19]Kierkegaard, *Point of View*.

[20]Ibid., 70.

[21]Abraham Heschel, *The Prophets* (New York: Harper, 1962), xvi.

[22]H. Diem, "Kierkegaard's Bequest to Theology," in *A Kierkegaard Critique*, ed. Howard Johnson and Niels Thulstrup (New York: Harper, 1962), 260.

[23]Holmer, *C. S. Lewis*, 35.

[24]Louis Mackey, *Kierkegaard: A Kind of Poet* (Philadelphia: University of Pennsylvania Press, 1971), 27–81.

[25]Kierkegaard, *Journals*, V, A, 47.

Chapter 6: *To a Proposal: The Experience of the Listener*

[1]Søren Kierkegaard, *Concluding Unscientific Postscript*, trans. David Swenson and Walter Lowrie (Princeton, N.J.: Princeton University Press, 1941), 116.

[2]Søren Kierkegaard, *Journals*, trans. Alexander Dru (New York: Harper, 1959), VI, A, 115.

[3]Erik Routley, *Into a Far Country* (London: Independent Press, 1962), 132.

[4]Susan Sontag, *Against Interpretation* (New York: Dew, 1966), 146.

[5]Fred B. Craddock, *As One Without Authority*, 4th ed. (St. Louis: Chalice Press, 2001); "Recent New Testament Interpretation and Preaching," *Princeton Seminary Bulletin* 66 (1973): 76–81.

[6]Walter Slatoff, *With Respect to Readers* (Ithaca, N.Y.: Cornell University Press, 1970), 37–38.

[7]Paul Holmer, *C. S. Lewis: The Shape of His Faith and Thought* (New York: Harper, 1976), 76.

[8]H. C. Gadamer, *Philosophical Hermeneutics*, trans. and ed. David Linge (Berkeley: University of California Press, 1976), xiv.

[9]W. A. Beardslee, *Literary Criticism of the New Testament* (Philadelphia: Fortress Press, 1970), 10–13.

[10]Routley, *Into a Far Country*, 31–32.

[11]Kierkegaard, *Concluding Unscientific Postscript*, 55.

Chapter 7: *To a Proposal: The Method of the Teller*

[1]I. A. Richards, *Principles of Literary Criticism* (New York: Harcourt Brace, 1961), 178.

[2]Robert McAfee Brown, "My Story and 'The Story,'" *Theology Today* 32 (1975): 166.

[3]Sallie [TeSelle] McFague, "Learning for the Whole Person: A Model from the Parables of Jesus," *Religion in Life* 45 (1976): 161.

[4]Søren Kierkegaard, *Concluding Unscientific Postscript,* trans. David Swenson and Walter Lowrie (Princeton, N.J.: Princeton University Press, 1941), 232.

[5]Walter Lowrie, *A Short Life of Kierkegaard* (Princeton, N.J.: Princeton University Press, 1942), 14.

[6]Stanley Fish, *Self-Consuming Artifacts* (Berkeley: University of California Press, 1972), xi.

[7]Stanley Fish, *Surprised by Sin: The Reader in Paradise Lost* (Berkeley: University of California Press, 1971) x.

[8]Augustine, *On Christian Doctrine,* Book 4.

Chapter 8: "Don't Be Afraid"

[1]The sermons "Don't Be Afraid," "The Bottom Line," and "Old Story, New Ending," were transcribed from audiotapes made at Cherry Log Christian Church (Disciples of Christ), Cherry Log, Georgia, where the sermons were preached.